The Busy Woman

Mary Hartley is a writer and personal development ~~~~~~~~
in people skills and communication. She has considerable experience of
writing on these topics and of presenting workshops and courses on aspects
of interpersonal communication and behaviour. As well as contributing to
national newspapers and women's and general-interest magazines, Mary
has broadcast on national and local radio programmes on issues such as
managing anger and coping with stress, and has acted as consultant for the
BBC Learning Zone. Her books *The Good Stress Guide, Managing Anger at
Work, Stress at Work, The Assertiveness Handbook* and *How to Listen so that
People Talk* are all published by Sheldon Press.

Overcoming Common Problems Series

Selected titles

A full list of titles is available from Sheldon Press,
36 Causton Street, London SW1P 4ST and on our website at
www.sheldonpress.co.uk

The Assertiveness Handbook
Mary Hartley

Cataract: What You Need to Know
Mark Watts

Cider Vinegar
Margaret Hills

Coping Successfully with Period Problems
Mary-Claire Mason

Coping with Age-related Memory Loss
Dr Tom Smith

Coping with Blushing
Professor Robert Edelmann

Coping with Bowel Cancer
Dr Tom Smith

Coping with Brain Injury
Maggie Rich

Coping with Candida
Shirley Trickett

Coping with Chemotherapy
Dr Terry Priestman

Coping with Gout
Christine Craggs-Hinton

Coping with Hearing Loss
Christine Craggs-Hinton

Coping with Heartburn and Reflux
Dr Tom Smith

Coping with Macular Degeneration
Dr Patricia Gilbert

Coping with Polycystic Ovary Syndrome
Christine Craggs-Hinton

Coping with Postnatal Depression
Sandra L. Wheatley

Depressive Illness
Dr Tim Cantopher

Helping Children Cope with Anxiety
Jill Eckersley

How to Approach Death
Julia Tugendhat

How to Be a Healthy Weight
Philippa Pigache

How to Keep Cholesterol in Check
Dr Robert Povey

How to Make Life Happen
Gladeana McMahon

How to Succeed in Psychometric Tests
David Cohen

How to Talk to Your Child
Penny Oates

Living with Heart Failure
Susan Elliot-Wright

Living with Autism
Fiona Marshall

Living with Fibromyalgia
Christine Craggs-Hinton

Living with a Seriously Ill Child
Dr Jan Aldridge

Living with Loss and Grief
Julia Tugendhat

Living with Rheumatoid Arthritis
Philippa Pigache

Losing a Child
Linda Hurcombe

Overcoming Hurt
Dr Windy Dryden

Simplify Your Life
Naomi Saunders

The Depression Diet Book
Theresa Cheung

The Multiple Sclerosis Diet Book
Tessa Buckley

The PMS Handbook
Theresa Cheung

The Thinking Person's Guide to Happiness
Ruth Searle

The Traveller's Good Health Guide
Dr Ted Lankester

Treat Your Own Knees
Jim Johnson

Treating Arthritis – The Drug-Free Way
Margaret Hills

Overcoming Common Problems

The Busy Woman's Handbook

MARY HARTLEY

First published in Great Britain in 2007

Sheldon Press
36 Causton Street
London SW1P 4ST

British Library Cataloguing-in-Publication Data
A catalogue record for this book is available from the British Library

ISBN 978-0-85969-996-9

1 3 5 7 9 10 8 6 4 2

Typeset by Fakenham Photosetting Ltd., Fakenham, Norfolk
Printed in Great Britain by Ashford Colour Press

Contents

1

The truth about time

Somewhere in your mind or hovering over your shoulder is a Superwoman. Details of her appearance are vague, but she looks perfect, with her make-up immaculate and her hair just so. Her clothes are clean, stylish and cleverly put together. She glows with health. She effortlessly juggles the demands of her crowded day, dealing with all the pressures of a busy family, work and social life, and organizing and controlling her time so that she achieves everything she wants to, including spending time on herself and the things she enjoys doing. She is a shining example of good time management for the woman of today.

Most of us aren't superwomen. We struggle to get through our packed schedules, constantly busy yet never quite getting there. We come to the end of the day exhausted, and don't know where the time has gone. We haven't stopped for a minute, but frequently feel that we have achieved little beyond just keeping our heads above water. Many of the things that we intend to do, or would like to do, are put on hold until we 'have more time'.

However, there is one thing that we all have in common with Super Time Manager: we all have the same amount of time in a day. We all have 24 hours, which is 1,440 minutes, or 86,400 seconds. This is the number of hours and minutes and seconds available to everyone. No one has the unfair advantage of an extra few hours; not even the richest person on earth can gain this. Time cannot be bought or borrowed. Those of us who are always late and those of us who are always punctual, those of us who find the time to keep in touch with distant friends and relatives and those of us who never have a minute to phone or write, those of us who are always 'too busy' and those of us who can always make time – every single one of us has just this number of hours in a day. No one has 'spare time', for the simple reason that spare time does not exist.

Of course, we talk about spare time, what we do in it and what we would like to do in it. We talk about it as if it were a tangible reality, something that will every now and again be tagged on to a regular day. This will never happen – there really is no such thing as spare time. We cannot conjure up an extra hour any more than we can clap our hands and create another room in our house. What we tend to call 'spare time' are the occasions when a gap in activity occurs, often unexpectedly. Then what we often do is fritter away this time because we have no clear idea of how to use it, or we are so relieved to stop that we just slump and later regret that we didn't do something with the time we have gained.

Just suppose that we did suddenly acquire more hours. Imagine a day that is, say, 30 hours long. Would that make a significant difference – or would we find that nothing changes, that the extra hours get filled up in just the same way, with the same never-ending list of things to be done and with the same levels of frustration and dissatisfaction?

We also talk about time as something that is wayward and elusive, that runs away with us, that has to be fought and controlled. Try instead to think of time as a gift: a precious gift that should be used with care and consideration. Time is an opportunity, the only opportunity we have, to do the things that matter to us and live the lives that we want to live. Too often we spend precious time doing the things that matter to other people, or the things that we feel we should be doing rather than the things that we want to do. The effect of this is that we can end up living someone else's life instead following our own path. We are affected by the persistent and often contradictory messages from society and the media about what women should be doing and how they should cope with the complex and pressing demands on their time. We become anxious about the choices that we make, guilty that we spend too much or too little time with partner, family, children, that we put too much or too little time into work and pursuing a career, guilty when we spend time on our own needs and desires and guilty when we don't.

Feeling guilty

Time crimes that we feel guilty about

'Wasting' time.
Spending time away from the children.

Not attending children's school functions.
Not exercising enough.
Not spending enough time with/on parents.
Not spending enough time with/on other family members.
Neglecting friends.
Spending too much time with friends.
Forgetting to return calls.
Forgetting to send cards for birthdays, exam successes, etc.
Spending too much time on the phone.
Not doing enough/anything for charity.
Not doing enough/anything for the environment.
Spending too much time on personal care.
Not spending enough time on personal care.
Having too many social activities.
Neglecting your social life.
Going out to work because you need the money.
Going out to work because you enjoy it.
Staying at home to look after children.
Not doing paid work because you don't need the money.
Missing deadlines.
Having to take time off because of something to do with your children.
Not being able to join in after-work activities because of family commitments.
Add your own ideas:

Where does this guilt come from?

Much of the guilt that we experience comes from uncertainty and lack of confidence about the roles that we play and how we fulfil them. We are driven by the thought that we should be good at everything, that we should be capable achievers in every area of our life, and that we are failures, at the very least in our own eyes, if we can't manage this.

What we expect of ourselves

The idea that women are nurturers and carers is central to many of the choices that we make about how we live our lives and spend our time. The deeply ingrained belief that our role is basically to support and see to the needs of others can make us feel guilty and inadequate, whatever the way in which we choose to interpret this part of our purpose in life. This may explain why any activities to do with our own personal needs are put at the bottom of the list, because we feel that we have no right to give them a higher priority. Time spent looking after ourselves is often called 'me time' or 'pampering time', as if it is a bolt-on luxury and something of an indulgence.

It actually isn't self-indulgent to consider your own needs. This is not the same as thinking only of your own needs – very few of us would want or be able to lead a totally self-centred life, free from all duties and obligations. But if you believe, or act as if you believe, that other people's claims on your time and their ideas about how you should use it are all that matter, you are neglecting the person at the core of all your activities, yourself.

When safety instructions are given on board an aircraft, we are told that should extra oxygen be required, we have to adjust our own masks before helping others. This is a helpful principle to bear in mind. Taking care of yourself is essential, and is what makes you able not only to care for others but to put your plans into effective action.

What others expect of us, and what we think others expect of us

We are surrounded by people who, in reality and in our imagination, have ideas about how we should or shouldn't spend our time. Often we are barely aware that we are taking in these messages and being influenced by them.

Some of the messages we respond to come from way back, from the ideas and opinions that we consciously or subconsciously absorbed from our family background. You may feel guilty when you do something your mother would never have done, such as not clearing up before you go out, or watching a daytime television programme. The mothers in your circle of friends and family can give guilt-inducing messages too, as you compare the quality of time and care they give their children with your style of parenting. We can be surprisingly susceptible to suggestions about our type of lifestyle. Even if we believe that we don't take any notice of magazine articles and television programmes about improving our environment and our appearance, they can creep into our consciousness and cause us to feel guilty and inadequate because the house looks like one of the 'before' examples in a house makeover programme, and we still haven't shifted the few extra pounds we gained the holiday before last.

Breaking free from the trap

The way to combat this guilt syndrome and break out of the trap of the overworked, overstretched cycle of activity is, first, to question the assumptions that are made about your roles and how you fulfil them, whether the assumptions are made by other people or by you yourself (see Exercise 1.1).

Exercise 1.1: How do other people influence your feelings about your use of time?

Person	Messages they give
Mother	_____
Father	_____
Spouse/partner	_____
Family members	_____
Friends	_____
Magazines and newspapers	_____
Television programmes	_____
People at work	_____
Add your own ideas:	_____
	_____
	_____

Unless anyone is actually harmed by your choices and preferences, there is no need to feel guilty about them, or that you 'should' or 'shouldn't' use your time in a particular way. Many of the expectations we have of ourselves are unrealistic and need to be brought into line with the reality of our lives and how we want to live them.

Identify your own needs and priorities

Stand back and analyse your own individual needs and the kind of life that you want. This involves establishing your personal priorities, the things that work for your own needs and circumstances. Getting this clear will stop you taking on too much, or worrying because you aren't doing enough.

Exercise 1.2: What I would do with more time

Choose activities from the following suggestions that reflect your wishes and your life plans, and add your own ideas.

Spend more time with my children
Spend more time with my partner
Go out with my partner
Talk to my partner
Find a partner
Go out with my friends
See more of family members
Email and phone friends and family
Make contact with people I regret losing touch with
Get on top of paperwork
Clean out the loft
Update my CV
Get some more qualifications
Update my IT skills
Look for another job
Keep the house clean and nice
Cook healthier meals
Clean the cooker
Watch television programmes that interest me
Listen to radio programmes that interest me

What would you do if you had more time (see Exercise 1.2)? Once you mange your time with a purpose, you will make available minutes, hours, days even that were previously spent in frantic activity which didn't actually get you where you wanted to be.

The key to managing time

Whatever your choices, good time management will help you to spend the hours at your disposal in ways that suit you. Time management is not about cramming more into an already over-crowded day. In fact, you cannot actually manage time at all. Nothing you do will make the hands on the clock move more slowly or more quickly. What you can do is manage yourself and the way that you use time. This is the key to good time management. It is

Decorate
Create a lovely garden
Catch up on my reading
Listen to music, go to concerts
Go to the cinema
Take dance classes
See exhibitions that interest me
Learn to play a musical instrument
Take long baths
Get a health check-up
Organize a once-in-a-lifetime holiday
Organize short breaks
Relax
Rent and watch DVDs
Personal care – hair, nails, etc.
Exercise or go to the gym
Take a course in something that interests me
Plan things rather than just let them happen
Do some kind of voluntary or community work
Join a choir or drama group
Shop for clothes
Add your own ideas: _____

_____

_____

about using well the time that we have, about spending the finite and limited hours and minutes at our disposal in the best possible way. It is about making choices that suit your individual needs and circumstances, choices that reflect your personality and support your plans and goals. It means keeping your focus on the things that matter to you, in every area of your life. When you achieve this, although you cannot affect the rate at which time moves, you will experience more of those occasions when time seems to fly by as you achieve what you want to and are engaged in what you are doing, and fewer of those occasions when every second seems an eternity.

Of course there will never be enough time to do everything you want. What you can do is develop some attitudes, skills and strategies to help you to make good choices, choices about your use of time

---

Exercise 1.3: Your attitude to time

		Yes	No
1	Do you spend your time the way that you want to?	☐	☐
2	Do you feel guilty because you don't get as much done as you think you should?	☐	☐
3	Do you always feel that you should be doing something to keep busy?	☐	☐
4	Do you always feel that you have too much to do?	☐	☐
5	Do you put off important jobs until the last minute and scramble to get them done on time?	☐	☐
6	Do you spend ages getting things just right?	☐	☐
7	Are you disorganized?	☐	☐
8	In the last month, have you forgotten anything important?	☐	☐
9	Do you know exactly where important documents such as your passport and insurance details are?	☐	☐
10	Do people often interrupt you?	☐	☐
11	Do you read every word of every document, memo, letter that you receive?	☐	☐
12	Do you spend ages checking your emails?	☐	☐

---

that will enable you to gain some control over where you direct your energy and to make space for the things that really matter to you and that you really want to do (see Exercise 1.3).

Some things that you will gain from managing time effectively

Putting first the things that matter most to yourself.
Finding more time to do what you want.
A sense of freedom.
A sense of being in control.
The ability to relax.
Less guilt.
Add your own ideas:

13 Do you use a calendar or diary? ☐ ☐

14 Do you make lists? ☐ ☐

15 Do you use the lists that you make? ☐ ☐

16 Do your lists reflect things that are important to you
    in every area of your life? ☐ ☐

17 Do you ever put items and documents somewhere
    'just for now'? ☐ ☐

18 Do you feel that you never have time for yourself? ☐ ☐

19 Do you ever feel guilty about the way that you
    use time? ☐ ☐

20 Do you set deadlines for getting things done? ☐ ☐

21 Do you feel that you have to do everything yourself? ☐ ☐

22 Do you spend time doing things and seeing people
    that have no real place in your life? ☐ ☐

23 Do you manage to find time for yourself? ☐ ☐

If you answered 'yes' to questions 1, 9, 13–16, 20, 23, and 'no' to
questions 2–8, 17–19, 21–22 you have some helpful time management habits already. Using time in a way that works for you and not
against you is a matter of developing habits of thought and behaviour that enable you to make good choices. You will need to make
some changes – but it will be worth it.

2

Spending time on what matters to you

Our lives are often so busy that we don't take a moment to ask ourselves what we are doing and why we are doing it. Constantly operating in 'survival mode' prevents us from standing back and focusing on what we want from our lives – and until this is done, we can have no idea about what good time management means for us as individuals. The first step to making time work for you is identifying and defining what matters to you (see Exercise 2.1). Once you are clear about your values and the kind of life you want you can make choices about how to spend your time effectively. After all, there is little point in saving time if you don't know what you are saving it for.

Exercise 2.1: Finding out what really matters

Try this way of defining what really matters to you. Imagine that you are going off on a long holiday at the end of today. You can only get three things done before you leave. Which three things will you choose?

1 _____

2 _____

3 _____

It is more than likely that putting the spice jars into alphabetical order would not be one of your top-priority tasks. Who knows, if you do this exercise every day, you may find that you lose the urge to do some of the tasks that take up your time now, and not only do they stop mattering to you, but you free up time to do something more pleasurable or life-enhancing.

Now try Exercise 2.2. You might have heard the saying that no one at the end of their life wished they had spent more time in the office. At the end of your life, what would you regret not having done?

Exercise 2.2: The life that you want

Imagine it's your hundredth birthday. At the celebration, someone makes a speech about you and your life. What kind of things would you like to be said? What qualities would you like your life to display? What achievements would you be proud of? Write them down here.

The values I would like my life to display: _____

_____

What I would be proud of: _____

_____

What I would regret: _____

_____

True values

Eve spends a lot of time on household tasks. She does not particularly enjoy these activities, but she has set herself certain standards and believes she must live up to them. They take a lot of time, and stop her from doing other things because she is 'too busy'. But at this special birthday, she does not want to be commended for her spotless bathroom and the hospital corners on every bed. She sees that she has not given time to the things that really matter to her.

Maggie gives a lot of time to her friends. She enjoys long chats, and evenings out, and maintains close relationships. She feels guilty because other things that she thinks she ought to be doing are neglected. However, she realizes that on her hundredth birthday she would like to be thought of as a good friend and listener who is a vibrant part of the lives of those she cares for. She knows there is no need to feel guilty; the way that she spends her time reflects what is important to her.

How do you spend your time at the moment?

There can be a difference between how we *think* we spend our time and how we *actually* spend our time. To check where the hours and minutes get to, keep a daily record of what you do (see Exercise 2.3 on p. 12). It would be useful to do this exercise for at least two days, even for a week, to see what kind of pattern emerges.

Exercise 2.3: Where does your time go?

Time	What I actually did
7.00–8.00	
8.00–9.00	
9.00–10.00	
10.00–11.00	
11.00–12.00	
12.00–13.00	
13.00–14.00	
14.00–15.00	
15.00–16.00	
16.00–17.00	
17.00–18.00	
18.00–19.00	
19.00–20.00	
20.00–21.00	
22.00–23.00	
23.00–24.00	

When you have a clear idea about how you spend your day, think about the proportion of time that you give to the things that really matter to you, and the proportion that you give to things that don't (Exercise 2.4). Of course, a certain amount of everyone's waking life is taken up with routine matters and with washing, eating, dressing, and there are demands that we have to meet; but what you can look for are the opportunities to save time by stopping some activities, and using the time that you reclaim to do things that you want to do.

What can go?

Many of us find that most of our time goes on routine activities and things that don't really matter. We may spend more time in conversation with acquaintances who mean little to us than we do with the important people in our lives; we may spend more time aimlessly thumbing through magazines and brochures than we do on reading material we positively enjoy. If you want to spend more time on fulfilling and focused activities, you have to get rid of something (see Exercise 2.5).

Exercise 2.4: Minutes that matter

Add up the number of minutes you spend doing things that reflect your values and what matters to you. Then add up the number of minutes you spend doing things that do not reflect your values and what matters to you.

Meaningful activities	Minutes	Non-meaningful activities	Minutes
1		1	
2		2	
3		3	
4		4	
5		5	
6		6	
7		7	
8		8	
9		9	
10		10	

Exercise 2.5: Activities that could go

Choose six activities that you could cut out or cut down on.

1
2
3
4
5
6

Setting goals

Once you know what is important to you and the values that you want to govern your life, you can start to formulate your own personal goals for living.

The idea of goal-setting can be daunting. Many of us have negative experiences of setting ourselves targets. Just think of all those new year resolutions that are abandoned around 7 January. Yet identifying goals is an essential step in learning to manage time effectively. People who have goals, and what's more write them down and use them as reference points, stand a much better chance of achieving their aims in life and using their time how they want to than those who don't identify what they want and where they are going. Your overall goals should be the focal point of all the decisions you make about how to allocate your time, because when you are clear about your ultimate aims you can assess the best use of your time.

Goals in balance

Make goals for all the important areas of your life. This may sound like a major task, but it is a good idea to focus on your life as a whole. Think of it as keeping your eye on all the balls that you are juggling. If you take your eye off a ball for too long, then events can overtake you. For example, if you ignore your overall health you could find that minor problems become bigger – a little toothache that you haven't got time to deal with becomes a major dental repair job, or you vaguely think that you will take more exercise 'one day', and then find that your lack of exercise is affecting your health. If you don't include the financial aspect of your life and just let your affairs drift on, you could find that not paying attention actually costs you money – you're late with credit card payments, for example, or you leave cash in an account that makes you very little interest because you never think to check current rates. You might, if asked, say that you and your partner go out together regularly, then realize that in fact it is six months or more since you actually did so. If we don't make a conscious effort to address all significant areas of our lives, we suffer the consequences of concentrating too much on one or two areas and ignoring the others.

You may think that there isn't enough time to spread round in this way. But you will find that once you establish your goals, not all of them require the same amount of time. You can choose to put most of your time and energy into the goals that matter most to you.

Some aims that you identify can be achieved with a very small time commitment. For example, keeping in touch with a distant friend or family member seems like a time-consuming demand until you think what it might mean: sending short regular emails (five minutes per message?) or phoning once every six weeks or so (15 minutes? – and see Chapter 10 for things that you can do while you're on the phone). Keeping an eye on your financial situation could take just a quarter of an hour each month. The biggest step is deciding to do it.

The process of setting goals for all aspects of your life is not as overwhelming as it sounds, because what you do is create your 'big picture' goals, then break them down into achievable parts. This is a manageable process that will help you to keep focused on the things that matter, and to manage time effectively and purposefully.

Create your 'big picture' goals

Don't think of your goals as targets that you *must* meet – the last thing you need is yet another pressure. Think instead that your goals are like snapshots or descriptions of the way you want your life to be. You can focus on the present, on a few years from now, or take a long-term view.

Your goals are descriptions of what you see happening in your life, what you want to maintain and what you want to develop. It might help to close your eyes and visualize yourself in different situations before you write them down.

See yourself at work, at home, with your family and friends. Choose a situation in turn. Visualize yourself behaving in the way that you want to, achieving the things that matter to you. Imagine yourself using your time in the way that you choose. Make the picture as big and as colourful and as vibrant as you can. Use your senses. What can you smell, see, touch, hear?

If you like, you could literally create a picture by putting together one or more montages that give a visual impression of your goals. Cut out pictures from papers and magazines, or draw your own. Use photographs. Include snippets of words and phrases that reflect what you are aiming for. Lines from songs and poems, film titles, quotations and sayings – copy them out, illustrate them. Play around with your images until you feel you have captured the essence of your life goals.

Give your goals deadlines

The word 'deadline' has a worrying ring, and you might immediately feel under pressure and that you need to hurry up and become even more busy to accomplish what you want. This is far from the case – but if you don't set yourself a timescale it is highly possible that you will let time drift by and won't actually do the things you plan. Knowing what you are aiming for will help you to focus on good use of your time. Remember that you are creating your own timescale, and you can adjust it if you need to, so make it work for you. You could work in timescales of six months, a year, five years, whatever suits your circumstances.

Write them down

Once you have established your goals, don't just keep them alive in your mind, write them down. It is essential to commit your goals and priorities to paper. Written goals are much more likely to be met than goals kept in our heads (see Exercise 2.6 on pp. 18–20).

Guidelines for writing down goals

Keep your written record visible. Put your goals in the notebook you use all the time, in your diary, on your computer, on cards, whatever you will look at frequently. Reminding yourself of what you are doing it all for will keep you focused.

Use the present tense. This springs you right into the situation you want to be in, and is an inspiring way of describing a goal. So, instead of 'I want to take the time to listen more carefully to my children', write 'I take the time to listen carefully to my children'. Instead of 'I will exercise three times a week', write 'I am exercising three times a week'.

Put everything in the positive. Thinking about what you will stop doing is part of the process of formulating your goals, but when you come to write them down, say what you *are* doing rather than what you are *not* doing. Instead of 'I have stopped wasting time just sitting in front of the television', say 'I choose the programmes that I enjoy and just watch those'.

Keep the big picture in mind

Hang on to the visions you have created. Don't worry if the picture changes. Goals can be altered as your circumstances change. What is appropriate for you at a particular stage of your life may not be applicable when your situation is different. Your core values will probably remain the same, but the ways in which you want your life to reflect them may change. Keep checking and revising as necessary, so that you adjust to and manage events rather than just let time roll on. Keeping the big picture in mind will help you to:

- Maintain focus on what really matters to you.
- Make decisions about your use of time – you can drop activities that don't support or develop your overarching goals.
- Make difficult decisions without guilt or anxiety.
- Say no.
- Ask for what you want.

Kate sees the big picture

Kate spends four evenings during the week and some of the week-end ferrying her children to various activities. She juggles car journeys between Brownies, Venture Scouts, ballet class, trampolining, drama group, netball, judo, extra swimming, band practice, guitar lessons, break-dancing class and French For Fun. Now Ben wants to learn tai chi, which will mean breaking into a fifth evening.

Kate is torn. She dislikes having no time during the week to devote to other matters, but at the same time she believes that her children benefit from the opportunity to take part in a range of activities. She feels trapped and resentful.

Kate is so caught up in the pressure and challenge of the arrangements and the difficulty of fitting everything in that she doesn't stop to ask if fitting everything in is the only option. She could ask herself this series of questions.

1 What is the big picture of what I want to do for the children and our family?
2 How do the current activities and the existing use of my time support the big picture?
3 To maintain the big picture, is it essential that every one of the current time demands is met?
4 How would the big picture be affected if not all of these demands were met?

Kate's answers reveal what the big picture is: her doing what she can

Exercise 2.6: Writing down your goals

Here are some typical life areas. Write your own brief goal description for each one. You can leave out sections and add ones of your own as you wish.

Family
Things to think about:
What kind of parent/brother/sister/daughter/son do I want to be?
What kind of relationship do I want with my family members?
What would I like more of and what would I like less of in my family life?
My big picture goal: _____
_____
_____

Significant other
Things to think about:
What kind of relationship do I have?
What kind of relationship do I want?
What would I like to be different about our life together?
What do I value in our life together?
How important is it to me to have a significant other in my life?
My big picture goal: _____
_____
_____

Friends and social life
Things to think about:
What kind of friend do I want to be?
What kind of friendships do I value?
Who do I like spending time with?
What would I like to spend more time doing?
What would I like to spend less time doing?
My big picture goal: _____
_____
_____

Paid work/career
Things to think about:
What aspects of my work are satisfying and fulfilling?

Are there aspects of the work itself or of situations at work that I find frustrating or difficult?
Am I sufficiently challenged?
How do I see my future?
What kinds of relationships do I have with people at work?
My big picture goal: _____

_____

_____

Financial health
Things to think about:
Am I in control of my financial situation?
Am I satisfied with my financial situation?
What could I do to make the financial area of my life run more smoothly?
Are there any financial arrangements I need to make?
My big picture goal: _____

_____

_____

Physical and mental health
Things to think about:
Do I have a healthy diet?
Are adjustments to be made to what I eat and drink?
Do I get enough exercise?
Do I look after myself?
What would I like to start doing?
What would I like to stop doing?
My big picture goal: _____

_____

_____

Spiritual or inner life
Things to think about:
Do I pay enough attention to this aspect of my life?
How do I rate my spiritual or inner well-being?
What would I like to start doing?
My big picture goal: _____

_____

_____

contd.

Exercise 2.6: contd.

Personal growth and development
Things to think about:
What new things would I like to learn?
What activities would I like to do regularly?
My big picture goal: _____

_____

_____

---

to help her children to be happy, well-rounded individuals, and to help their family to be close and to enjoy each other's company. Her children's involvement in extra-curricular activities contributes to their development. However, Kate sees that if the present arrangements were altered and the children did fewer activities, and did them at times that suited her needs as well, the big picture would not suffer. In fact, the quality of their family life would improve because she would gain more time and be less stressed. (Go to Chapter 5 to see how Kate uses a decision-making process to help her to make these time-saving changes.)

The myth of having it all

You need to check your big goals and make sure that they are workable. You might have to negotiate with and consult other people who are involved in your plans or affected by them – you will run into difficulties if you have plans that significant people in your life are firmly opposed to. Check too that your goals don't conflict with each other and cancel each other out. Don't attempt to achieve everything you want just because you want it. Chasing the impossible is the cause of stress and frustration and is a great waste of time.

Be realistic. Some aspirations are mutually exclusive. You can't be there for your children after school every day *and* do a job that finishes at six o'clock; you can't go off travelling for six months *and* be the main carer for a family member. Your finances may also affect what you can achieve. You might have to delay or change your plans until your circumstances enable you to pursue them.

Make your big picture specific

You need now to narrow down your broad plans in order to make them more specific.

Jacintha makes a date
Part of Jacintha's big picture is 'spend more time with my partner'. She recognizes that in the course of a busy week days can go by when they hardly see each other, let alone have any meaningful communication. She narrows down her broad goal into a specific aim: 'Go out with David once a week, and talk to each other without distractions for ten minutes every evening.'

Exactly how much time is 'more time with the children'? How often would you like to have a night out with your friends? What does 'personal care' mean – doing your nails, having a manicure, getting your hair cut and highlighted or just getting a chance to have a bath without being interrupted?

This is where many new year resolutions fail. We decide to 'lose weight' or 'get fit' without setting precise, attainable goals. A resolution that states, for instance, 'lose 10 pounds in 6 weeks', or 'walk to work twice a week', stands more chance of being kept (see Exercise 2.7).

Exercise 2.7: Making goals specific

Choose five or six aims that are realistic, achievable and reflect the way that you want to use your time. Set yourself a deadline for each one – this increases your chances of actually doing it.

	Big picture goal	Specific aim	By when
1	_____	_____	_____
2	_____	_____	_____
3	_____	_____	_____
4	_____	_____	_____
5	_____	_____	_____
6	_____	_____	_____

Barriers to achieving your aims

Every day we encounter obstacles that prevent us from putting into practice our good intentions. Some of these barriers are external, and some of them come from within ourselves. Some things that drain our time include:

> Being disorganized.
> Not having a plan.
> Taking on too much.
> Not finishing what you start.
> Being interrupted.
> Taking too long over everything.
> Not having the appropriate skills.
> Putting things off.
> Doing everything yourself.
> Being easily distracted.
> Not saying what you mean.
> Not listening.
> *Add your own ideas:*

Moving forward

The good news is that we can develop skills to overcome these obstacles. You can learn ways of freeing up time to enable you to take control of your activities and channel your energy to achieve the things that matter to you.

3

Planning how to use your time

Once you have a clear idea of your goals, you can think about how to translate them into actions that will help you to live the life you want to live. What you need to do is look at the big picture that you have created and work out how to use your time in actions that support these goals. Planning is important. If you don't plan how to use your time you are unlikely to use it in the way that is most productive for you.

However, your plan doesn't need to be too detailed, and you don't need to spend that much time planning. There is a theory called the Pareto Principle, which can be applied to all areas of our lives. An Italian economist called Vilfredo Pareto estimated that 80 per cent of results comes from 20 per cent of input. This means that for 20 per cent's worth of effort you get 80 per cent's worth of results. In other words, it's not the amount of time you spend doing things that makes a difference, it's doing the right things. So spending just a few minutes planning will bring you benefits in much greater proportion than the time that you put in.

Make your plans

When to do it

You don't need to be sitting down with a pen and paper to plan and think ahead. Sometimes ideas come into your head when you are going for a walk, having a bath or driving to work. It is important, though, to set aside some time. Just ten minutes would be enough.

What to do

Begin by putting everything down on paper. Write down everything that is on your mind, all the things that you need to do. Include the big picture things, and all the little niggles and reminders that are nagging away at you as well. Don't think about timescales or about the relative importance of different items – just unburden yourself and get it all out of your mind and on to paper. Don't worry when you end up with a list that looks overwhelming.

It is important to write down this list and not to rely on your memory – one or two items are bound to slip your mind. Also, when items are written down it stops you worrying about trying to remember. It is a first step to actually getting on with things.

Melanie's Big List
Melanie's list looks like this:
Decorate hall, stairs and landing.
Buy a new computer.
Do all ironing in basket.
Defrost the fridge.
Tell Martin we can't make the 7th.
Get hair cut.
Renew insurance.
Buy garden plants.
Start project for my course.
Make packed lunches.
Email Jane.
Phone my mother.
Find out train times to Brighton.
Ring plumber.
Ask Sue to swap shifts.
Organize summer holiday.

Turn your plans and projects into specific actions

Your Big List (see Exercise 3.1) is like your map of how to get to your goal. At this point it may look a little daunting. However, nothing can be achieved in one fell swoop; every project we take on is a series of steps, with each step taking you nearer to your destination. Big things on Melanie's list, such as the decorating project, can be broken down into a series of steps, such as choosing paint, phoning for quotes, etc. Just one of these steps moves her project forward and means that she is actually doing something towards achieving it.

So what you do is break down the items on your list into single actions that you can achieve. Your ultimate goals are made up of

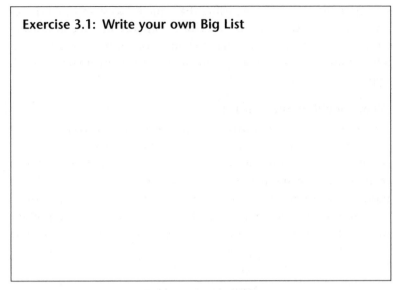

Exercise 3.1: Write your own Big List

individual actions, and each single action will take you nearer your goal. What you have to do now is to identify the next action you need to take to move your plan forward. When you have made a list of single actions, even the most worrying task begins to look achievable.

Make your 'to do' list

A central tool of time management is a 'to do' list which itemizes and prioritizes the tasks that you plan to complete each day. There are computer programs that can set this out for you, but even if you have such a facility it could be more useful to have a written list that you can keep with you. If you like using a personal electronic organizer you will find it very good for this process.

The list should be accessible and visible. The idea is that you update it as you go. When tasks are done you tick them or cross them through, and add items as they occur. This might sound as if you will have loads of 'must do's' weighing you down and adding to your guilt when you don't get them done. However, you can work your list so that it is liberating rather than constraining. Use it to remind yourself to do the things that matter. When you write down your intention to get your hair cut, to meet a friend, to read two chapters of your book, using the same list as your other duties and responsibilities, you consolidate the importance of committing time to everything that matters to you. Look on this list not just as a list of tasks, but as a working document for organizing and developing your life.

What should go on your list

A working 'to do' list consists of single actions that you need and want to accomplish. Rather than saying 'organize party', your list should remind you to 'phone caterers' or 'write invitations'. Some of these will be more important than others, and some will be more urgent than others. Make sure the actions that fall into these categories have a time schedule – but if something isn't important to you and there is no urgent need to do it, don't waste valuable time writing it down as a commitment.

How to prioritize

Arrange the things on your 'to do' list into different categories according to how important they are.

Category Red

In this category put really important things that matter and that have to be done. These are tasks that are central to your life, to the different roles that you fulfil and to your goals. They are the activities that contribute to the goals you are aiming for, whether they are to do with your personal life or your working life. If you are going to do only one thing today, it should be something from this category.

Sometimes you can choose to do these tasks, while at other times you have no choice: there is a deadline you have to meet, or an emergency crops up and you have to drop everything to deal with the matter.

If this category becomes overloaded, you can end up having one of those days, or weeks or months, when it seems that you do nothing except fight against time to get things done.

Leanne's Category Red day

Leanne has lots of things that she wants to get done today, including three urgent and important items, activities that contribute to her big picture goals:

1 Do report for work – due in at the end of today.
2 See Harry play in the school concert.
3 Fill in and submit job application – deadline tomorrow.

She has scheduled time for completing the report and the job application before attending the school concert, but they each take much longer than she had thought, and other things crop up during the day as well. In the end she has to settle for being a little late with the report, and even then she only just makes the concert on time.

The way to avoid getting into this situation is to use the next category for planning and getting ahead of yourself.

Category Green

In this category put the really important things that matter but do not need to be done straight away. Some tasks are important but not urgent – although they matter to you and have an impact on your life, they do not have a deadline and no one will chase you to make sure that they are done. These are activities that we tend to put off until we have 'more time', with the consequence that they don't get done at all, or they are put off until they become urgent, at which point they join all the items sitting in the Red category, adding to the pressure of your already crowded day.

One of the secrets of effective time management is to make space every day to do things that matter, even though they are not technically urgent; no one will notice if you don't do them, and they can always be put off until another day. Writing them on your list is a pledge that you will make space and time to do them. Give these activities your own deadline and treat them as if they were urgent. Below are some examples of Green category items which don't have deadlines:

Activities to do with your personal needs and your personal development

Your daily list may contain items such as 'make dental appointment' for yourself or for family members, but 'book evening out' or 'have swim' or 'find out about art class' may not get written down, because they are the kinds of activities you squeeze in 'if there is time'. If it matters to you, write it on your list, and decide when you will do it.

Shona's personal priority

Shona notices that Pilates classes are being held on Wednesday evenings in her local community centre. She would really like to take these classes, and thinks that she will go along one Wednesday and enrol. The weeks go by, and she doesn't get round to it – until she writes on her Wednesday 'to do' list '7 p.m. Go to Pilates'. The action of writing it down, and the constant reminder of her intention every time she consults her list during the day, increase the likelihood of her actually doing it. If Shona for some reason did not go along to the class on that day she could carry forward the item to the next week, writing it down in advance and making it a high priority. If she found that she was having to carry it forward yet again, Shona might ask herself if her desire to attend the class was in fact that strong in the first place.

Activities to do with personal relationships

Sometimes we think that we spend time with and on our friends and families. But if we had to be specific, we might admit that in fact we do not spend significant time with our children, or that weeks can go by without our having a satisfying chat or meeting with a friend.

Family time

Write down what you want to do: read a story to Leah; leave work at 5.30 p.m.; take Jack to swimming. If you don't identify and write down the actions that you want to take, you will put them off; time slips by and you realize that you haven't seen your youngest at bedtime for a year or had a conversation with your partner about anything other than the children or the washing-up for two weeks or more.

Social activities

If you find that you are constantly thinking 'I really must give so-and-so a ring', or 'I must meet so-and-so for lunch before the holidays', then write it down on your list: 'Ring Louise'; 'Choose three dates and ring Janet'.

Thinking and planning time

Often we just need time to think through something that is on our mind – how to handle a difficult relationship, how to ask for a raise at work. Projects such as holidays or home improvements need thought and planning. Schedule time to do your preliminary thinking, discussing and planning. By writing it down on your daily list you are giving this activity the priority it deserves. Taking time to plan is a way of saving time in the future.

Little bites

This is where you include the actions that will move on your big tasks. By taking little bites at a big project you eventually get it done, and in time. You might think that it is a waste of time to do things when they don't actually need to be done, but in fact it is good insurance against the unpredictable, as well as a way of making daunting tasks manageable. If Leanne had planned ahead, she would have stood more chance of completing her Category Red items. She left herself with a day when she really had 'no time' for anything else – not a good idea because we never know what a day is likely to throw at us. Doing the bulk of or at least starting the job application and the report in advance, before the deadline was imminent, would have helped Leanne to complete her tasks on time.

Category Blue

Category Blue items do not *need* to be done at once, but we treat them as urgent. The reason that we do these tasks before other more central ones is that they demand our attention, or we convince ourselves that they are more important then they really are. Tasks in this category include ones that we have to do, or choose to do, because someone else needs us to do them. They become urgent, with a tight deadline, because they are urgent to another person.

I need it now!

Tanya has had a very frustrating day. At work, she couldn't get on with what she had planned because people kept interrupting her with requests. She had to do a load of photocopying for Geoff, who plonked it on her desk and said he needed it done right away, then Marisa asked her to dig out some statistics for a report she needed to get finished by the end of the morning. Just as she was beginning to get somewhere with her own work, Tanya stopped what she was doing to spend 20 minutes showing Lee how to use the new software program. When she got home, Josh met her with, 'I need my football kit washed for tomorrow', and Hannah called out, 'I need a lift to Susie's house because we've got to work on our project.' Tanya feels that she has been busy all day but has not been able to focus on her own priorities.

What we need to do, if we are constantly faced with these kinds of time demands, is decide where we draw the line between being helpful and allowing people to impose on our time. If you find that you are often interrupted and have to put your own priorities on hold, think about ways of lessening the interruptions. You will find some suggestions in Chapter 5.

Category Pink

Actions that are not urgent, and don't actually move things on, but are often nice to do, go in this category. Some activities aren't really important and don't *need* to be done, but they are things we enjoy doing. Many of our soothing or settling rituals fall into this category. The social phone call that drifts on and on pleasantly and pointlessly, reading an article about how to keep weeds at bay when you haven't even got a garden, having another cup of coffee that you don't really need, in fact anything that prevents us from doing the things that matter.

Spending your time on activities that do not contribute to your big picture goals is a waste of time – be brave and ditch them. Don't do things that use up your time and stop you from getting on with the life that you want.

At the same time, we all need a bit of soothing. It is not good practice to spend valuable time on trivial activities, but sometimes tidying a drawer or sharpening all the pencils or watering the plants can actually give you a surge of energy to tackle the real stuff. Don't give these activities a high priority, though; just have them on hand for the odd unexpected spare moment, or when such an activity is the very thing that you need at that point.

Keep a note of these types of unimportant things that might be fun or useful or satisfying to do some time, and use them as treats for yourself.

How to arrange your list

Our natural instinct is to write items one underneath the other, which leads us to try to work through them methodically, but this might mean that we lose sight of high-priority items. When the day is over we have lots of satisfying ticks to show how much we have achieved, without realizing that the ticked-off items are not the most important or significant ones.

A system that highlights your top-priority items is a good idea. You could put these activities together at the top of your list. Or you could try a star system, marking important and urgent items with four stars and grading others accordingly. Colour coding can give you an immediate visual indication of important items (see Exercise 3.2).

Exercise 3.2: Prioritizing what you have to do

Write down all the things that you want to achieve tomorrow. Decide into which category each task falls. Mark each task Red, Green, Blue or Pink. You could use different coloured pens or paper to differentiate between the items.

It might work for you to group similar items. How you group them is up to you – make your list your own personal working document. You might clump items under specific projects, or under type of activity, so that you put all the reminders about phone calls together, and group all the actions to do with finding information, and so on.

Another strategy is to group actions according to where you will do them. Put together all the things that you can do in town, all those that you need to do on your computer, all the things that can be done in the kitchen and all the items that you can do at the library, and so on.

Try putting together items that you will do at particular times of the day. Group together the things you will do in the morning, and list together your after-work or evening tasks. This means that a top-priority item might actually appear at the bottom of the page, but as long as you have clearly marked it and know when you will do it, this doesn't matter at all.

What to use for your list

It's a good idea to use one continuous list that keeps all your reminders together. Don't use odd bits of paper that are likely to get separated and lost. Diaries and notebooks, paper and electronic, work well, as do loose-leaf pages kept in a personal organizer. You need plenty of space for notes and jottings. Try a system that helps you to plan in advance. A blank page for every week, either in the appropriate place in your diary or just dated, will allow you to slot actions into the proper place in advance. When you turn over the pages of your book, you see already in place the reminders of what you need to do at that point.

Choose a notebook or diary that is the right size for you to have with you all the time, and is easy to handle. Whatever system you develop, make it one that you enjoy using. You are going to be consulting it every day, so make this action one of the first pleasures of the day.

When to make the list

A 'to do' list should be made every day. It's a good idea to date it. Start by scanning the previous day's list and carrying over any items that have not been ticked off – if they really do need to be done.

The best time to draw up your list is the night before. It focuses your mind on how you might make the best use of your time the next day, and also the very act of writing down all that you have to do helps you to put these things out of your mind so that you can relax and get a good night's sleep. Also, you never know what the morning will bring so it is good to be as prepared as you can be.

When you will do things – establishing time slots

Feeling that we have too much to do can often make us panic when something else appears on our agenda – even if that something is a pleasant and welcome activity.

> Lorna's friend Susie phones her. 'How about getting together one evening next week? We could go for a meal, or just have a drink if you prefer. It's ages since we've had a good chat.'
>
> Lorna would love to see Susie, and has in fact been thinking that she hasn't seen her for a long time. 'I'd like that,' she says. In her mind she runs through the coming week. There's a parents' meeting at school one evening, then there's badminton which she can't get out of because it's a league game, and she needs to give the house a thorough clean before Geoff's parents come at the weekend, and if they run on to the following week, well, it's the same again really and there's just loads to do 'But I don't think I can,' she says. 'I've just got so much on.'

One way of avoiding a reaction like Lorna's is to put into your week a structure that makes it easier for you to accommodate different kinds of demands. Try this with some of the activities that you need to do and want to do, ones that do not have a designated time slot but just get fitted in when you can. These might include:

> Meeting friends.
> Household chores.
> Dealing with paperwork.
> Personal emails.
> One of your interests or hobbies.
> Spending time with children.
> Spending time with your partner.
> *Add your own ideas:*

Now look at the pattern of your week. You will have blocks of time, such as your working hours and other fixed commitments, which are accounted for. There will be other pockets of time that are not actually accounted for, although of course they always

get filled up. This happens because we don't think of undesig-
nated hours as time that can be used for specific purposes of our
choice, so we fritter them away, or allow other people to fill them
up for us. A better system is to identify time slots that you could
dedicate to some of your chosen activities (see Exercise 3.3).

> Lorna does not have a regular commitment on Thursday evenings.
> She realizes that she could designate 8 p.m. onwards as her time for
> meeting or phoning friends. This does not mean that she has to spend
> every single minute of the time slot in this way, but it means that the
> time is protected and reserved for this particular activity. Not only does
> this enable her next time to say to Susie, 'How about Thursday?', it also
> stops that internal nagging along the lines of 'I really must phone', etc.
> Once she knows that Thursday is her time for catching up with these
> things she can be more relaxed.

Having a regular slot for household chores is a good way of keeping on top of them and knowing that they will get done. If you
schedule cleaning the kitchen floor for before you leave for work
on a Wednesday you don't have to keep thinking 'I must clean that
floor', because you know when it will be done.

Time slots can be short. You can decide to devote just 10 or 15
minutes to something.

Match the activity and the time with your own preferences and
energy levels. For instance, if you are an early riser and always feel
alert first thing in the morning, you might find a regular slot at
this time to deal with paperwork. This might suit you much better
than trying to fit it in at the end of a day when you are tired and
unable to concentrate. Again, knowing that you will be sending
off those bills or checking bank statements at a certain time stops
that nagging at the back of your mind.

Be flexible

Don't think of the plan as a rigid timetable. It's a method of finding
time to do the things that you want to do, and provides you with a
structure that will help you to fit in all your various demands. Use
it so that it helps you and takes away some of the pressure. Make
changes when you want to. Swap activities and times around until
you have a system that works well for you.

Top tip for time slotting

Don't go over your allocated time. If you say that you are going to spend ten minutes or half an hour doing something, don't let it drift on. It's surprising how much you can get done when you work to a time limit.

Exercise 3.3: Identifying time slots

Choose six activities that you would like to find time for. Identify time slots that you could dedicate to these activities. You could work on a weekly or monthly pattern.

	Activity	Day	Time
1	_____	_____	_____
2	_____	_____	_____
3	_____	_____	_____
4	_____	_____	_____
5	_____	_____	_____
6	_____	_____	_____

Doubling-up activities

Try to find ways of getting more than one aim accomplished at the same time. If you enjoy cooking and would like to try out new dishes, but feel that you haven't got time to do this and spend some time with the children as well, get them to join in and help you to cook. If you really need to iron, do it while you are chatting to someone, or taking in radio or television programmes that are on or that you have recorded to watch at this particular time (see Exercise 3.4 on p. 36).

Even the routine activities of getting ready in the morning can be enriched if you do them in a way that focuses on your overall aims. Depending on your own choices, you could:

Get up early enough to meditate or sit quietly for ten minutes.
Get up early enough to exercise for ten minutes.
Enhance your personal care needs by choosing toiletries and products that you enjoy using and which make you feel good.

Listen to the news while you get ready.
Listen to music while you get ready.
Talk to someone while you get ready.
Say something nice to someone.

Exercise 3.4: Doubling-up activities

Think of ways in which you can achieve two or more aims through one activity.

Activity	*What it achieves*
1 _____	_____
2 _____	_____
3 _____	_____

Useful planning tools

The value of a notebook

A notebook will answer many of your needs. It needs to be handy enough to carry around but substantial enough to be useful. Take the time to find one that you really like using. Ones that are ring-bound or have pages with perforated edges are handy because you can easily tear out pages when you have finished with them, or you could choose to use a loose-leaf organizer. You may like to use a PalmPilot or a BlackBerry or a similar electronic organizer – the principles for using them are the same.

When you have found a notebook that works well for you, buy in a stock of them. It's worth geting a pen or pens that are nice to write with. Pens with retractable tips are a good idea because you don't have to fumble with caps and remember to put them back on. Choose a nib width that suits your own handwriting and the size of notebook that you prefer. A broad-nibbed pen doesn't work well if you are writing in a small book, unless you write only one or two words per page. Getting this right really makes a difference to the ease with which you write and later read what you have written.

Use your notebook for jotting down all the things you may later wish you had made a note of. When people pass on the name of a shop or a restaurant, or a good plumber, or you come across the name of a website that you would like to explore, write it down in your notebook. This will save all the time you spend trying to track it down later. You can write down the odd ideas and thoughts that float into your mind and would be good to capture before they float out again. It's also helpful to keep in your notebook a list of references that may be useful to have when you are out of the house. (More about this in Chapter 4.)

You might like to use the same book for your 'to do' list, with the front half dedicated to reminders of what you want to do and pages towards the back kept for the other purposes.

Planners and calendars

Apart from a notebook, you might also find a planner or calendar useful. There are no hard and fast rules – what is important is to find a system that works for you and runs smoothly so that you use your time in the best possible way.

A planner could stay in the same place – by the phone, in the kitchen, wherever suits you – or you might prefer one that you always carry with you. A family-type calendar could go somewhere like the kitchen wall. Choose one which has a column for each family member. This enables you to see at a glance who has a dental appointment, a football practice, a sleepover and so on. It is also good for spotting clashes that might mean a time commitment for you. You could get people to write in their own information; you could colour code it so that you can see at a glance who's doing what when. It's best to use just one visible calendar for everything. Block out regular activities, working hours, times when you won't be available. There are computer programs that do this kind of planning for you, if you prefer, or want a back-up.

Bringing it all together

Apply the strategy in Exercise 3.5 to all your goals. Just ask yourself, 'What single thing do I need to do next to move this along?' Commit yourself to doing it by a certain date. Sooner or later, there will be no next thing. You're there!

Exercise 3.5: Bringing your Big List to heel

Go back to the list that you made earlier.

For every item on your list, write down a series of single actions, or even just one action.

Decide which category the actions fall into.

Decide when you will do them.

Write each one down in the appropriate place.

Now you have a list of things you can do next, and you don't have to worry about remembering all that you have to do.

4

Make it easy for yourself: time-saving habits

Sometimes our time gets eaten away and everything takes longer than it should because we have drifted into habits and ways of doing things that are not productive. The solutions are often obvious, it's just that we haven't taken the time to think about how making one or two changes to our usual routines could save us time and energy.

Adopting good habits

Be in the right place for what you are doing

You may have tasks and activities that end up taking longer than they should, or which you end up tackling at a time of day that does not suit you, because the place in which you do them does not feel comfortable. It is much easier to do things quickly, even things we dislike doing, if the environment is comfortable, pleasant and appropriate to the task. Sometimes just a small adjustment is all that is necessary to prevent you from putting off particular tasks, or doing only half as much as you planned to (see Exercise 4.1, p. 40).

> ### The cold study
> Anna likes to deal with the household paperwork in her small study, where there is a small desk and comfortable chair, and filing space. However, Anna puts off going into the study, and leaves letters and documents on various surfaces around the house, so that they pile up and sometimes get lost. What should be matters of routine maintenance turn into time-consuming tasks.
>
> When Anna thinks about why this happens, she realizes that it is because the study is always chilly. This makes her reluctant to go in there, and when she does she rushes through and leaves things half-finished. Anna gets a small heater for the room, and the comfort that this provides enables her to make her system work.

Exercise 4.1: Getting the right place

List the activities that you put off or don't do properly because you are not comfortable in the place in which you do them. Think of changes you could make.

	Activity	Place	What's wrong	Change I could make
1	_____	_____	_____	_____
2	_____	_____	_____	_____
3	_____	_____	_____	_____
4	_____	_____	_____	_____
5	_____	_____	_____	_____

Have the things you need in the right place

There will be some situations and places you can identify where you always have a few minutes to spare – not enough time to do anything major, but just enough to do one of those little tasks that need to get done. Sometimes it is quicker to dash off small things, like writing cheques or filling in reply coupons, in moments and places like these, rather than at your desk or wherever it is you do such activities.

Try using a little container, something like an old chocolate box or toiletries gift box, or an attractive basket, to keep to hand a supply of pens, paper, envelopes, cards and stamps. You could include a cheque book. Keep it in a place where you are likely to have just a few minutes in which you could write a cheque, or write, address and stamp a congratulations or get well card. This system might work for you by having the box in the kitchen, for those spare moments when you wait for the kettle to boil, or on the hall table where you always have to wait a few minutes for everyone to be ready to leave, or within reach when you watch television and can deal with these tasks while you watch a programme or during the commercial breaks.

Remember what you need

The best-laid plans come unstuck when we don't have what we need to hand. If you added up all the hours and minutes you lose because of items you have forgotten or misplaced, you would probably uncover enough time to do one of the nice things that you never have time for!

The frustration of forgetting

Corinne is doing a part-time degree course. She has planned to spend an hour in the college library after work. When she gets to the library she realizes that the reference list she needs is at home on the kitchen table. She had been so frazzled getting herself and the children out of the house that she forgot to put the list in her bag.

A way of preventing this happening is to stop at the front door before you leave, no matter how rushed or late you are, and pause for just the few seconds it takes to do a mental run-down of the items you need. The mantra 'tickets, passport, money' is routinely chanted in many households at holiday time; create your own chant to suit your circumstances.

A good way to focus on what you need is to create a quick visualization of what you will be doing during your day. This need take only half a minute. If Corinne had created a mental picture of herself travelling, working and then being in the library, the picture of herself consulting her reference list in the library would have triggered her memory.

Use your memory

Writing things down is a great habit, and it will save you time. Back this up with improved memory skills, and you need never forget anything again!

How to remember a list of items

Try this visualizing exercise. Suppose you need to buy milk, a pack of felt-tip pens for your daughter's homework and a top-up for your mobile phone. You are going to imagine a tour of your house, with these items scattered along the way in places that make them stand out.

Shut your eyes and imagine yourself in the living room of your house. In your mind, place the milk somewhere in the room. It might be on top of the television. Now see yourself going out of the door towards the next room. On your way, you pass the pack of felt-tip pens, right in the middle of the hall so that you almost fall over it. Go into the next room. In your mind, see your mobile phone hanging on the wall, framed like a picture.

When you get to the shops, imagine yourself going through your house, taking the milk off the television, picking up the pens and taking the phone off the wall. The combination of the familiar layout of your house and the prominence of these odd objects works as a memory trigger. You can use this technique to remember a long list of items – just keep going round your house!

Another trick you might try is to take the first letters of everything that you need to remember and use them to create a phrase of your own. So if you want to remember milk, pens, phone, take the letters M, P, P and make a sentence like 'My Pet Puppy' or 'Mother Pops Pills'. Make the phrase one that you won't forget. As you repeat the phrase to yourself, you remember the item that each letter stands for.

How to remember your pin number

Save time and hassle by having a back-up way of remembering your pin or other important numbers. This trick works in the same way as the previous one, by giving each number from 1 to 9 a letter, using the first nine letters of the alphabet. So A is 1, B is 2 and so on. If your pin is 9721, you have the letters I, G, B, A, which could become a phrase like 'I've Got By Again'. If you remember words more easily than numbers, try finding a rhyme for each digit, e.g. one = fun, two = shoe, and so on.

Make it easy to find what you need quickly

Something as simple as paying a bill or wrapping a birthday present can take ages if you have to go into another room to get an envelope, then wander around asking who last used the scissors, then embark on an expedition to find postage stamps. This familiar situation is caused partly by not having the right things in the right place, and partly by things having a right place but being put elsewhere. Of course, the obvious solution is to always put things back where they should be, but even if you are disciplined enough to do this it is unlikely that everyone in your household will follow suit.

Double-up supplies

A time-saving answer to this might be to double-up on supplies. For example, you might need to use scissors in the kitchen, in the office or study area, in the bedroom or wherever you get dressed (to do things like cutting off price tags and snipping stray threads), and in the place where you read newspapers and magazines (to cut out items of interest). A pair of scissors in each room would save time and save your stress levels as well.

Try keeping a tin opener with the cans as well as with the utensils. Buy three extra umbrellas and put one near the door, one with your coat and one in the car. Keep cleaning materials on every floor of your house.

How about keys? Many of us have our own keys and a spare set, which we are reluctant to use in case they get lost as well. One or more extra sets, strategically placed, will save time, and in fact once you know that they are available, it is unlikely that you will ever have to use them. A strategic place for spare car keys might be actually on your person, in your bag. (See Exercise 4.2.)

Exercise 4.2: Doubling-up items

Think of situations in which you would save time by having extra supplies of items available. Then put them on your shopping list straight away.

Extra item/s	Where it/they will go	How I will save time
e.g. Spare lipstick	Glove compartment	It will take just 30 seconds to repair my appearance
Pens	Within reach of phone, PC, kitchen table	No need to hunt around for a pen
Keys		

Put items where they are needed

Keeping items in the place where they are actually used saves you time going from room to room. Put a corkscrew with the wine bottles. Put your make-up bag in the place where you always apply your make-up. If it is a hassle getting into the bathroom or wherever you do this, put a mirror somewhere else and use that spot.

Make items accessible

It's a good idea to have the items that you use regularly within easy reach. So it only takes a minute to move the juicer that you never use to get hold of the coffee grinder that you use every day, and it takes no time at all to get behind the pile of shoes that you don't wear to locate your favourite boots – but all these little bits of time add up, and you will feel more comfortable and in control if everyday activities run smoothly and quickly.

Don't lose things

Looking for items that we have lost is such a frustrating waste of time. Take steps to minimize the occasions when this happens, because when you don't have to clutter up your mind and your time searching for things you will find that life becomes more relaxed and streamlined. You will feel more in control and you will find time that you didn't know you had.

How not to lose things

Establish this simple two-part system:

- Decide where you will keep each item.
- Always put everything back in the right place.

Of course, this system won't always be followed, but it does give you a basis to work on. It will help you to track down a lost item, because an item in the wrong place is likely to be conspicuous, and this will help you to visualize where you last saw it.

If you do have to search for something you need, give yourself a time limit. Depending on what it is, decide to spend 5, 10 or 15 minutes looking for it, and if you don't find it, then forget about it and do something else. This has two benefits. First, when you put something out of your mind, quite often what happens is that your subconscious mind kicks into gear and you suddenly remember where you put the invitation, or your glasses, or the letter about the school trip. Second, if you launch into a thorough search and spend ages on it, you are likely to get distracted by all the other things you come across, which may be great fun but perhaps not the way you want to use your time at this point.

Shopping

Shop the time-saving way

If you spend a lot of time shopping, think about what aspects of it you enjoy and what elements you would like to get rid of. You may find that shopping for basics is boring and time-consuming, while shopping for 'extras' or for personal items is enjoyable. Think about allocating your time so that you make room for opportunities to browse and shop in a leisurely way, and find a different system for buying the mundane and day-to-day items.

Buy in bulk

Depending on how much storage space you have – no one wants to feel that they are sharing their home with giant packs of toilet rolls – always buy more than one of the items you buy regularly, and halve the time you spend shopping for them. Stock up on items such as canned goods, light bulbs, toiletries, washing powders, cleaning materials. Even if you haven't got much room, it should be possible always to store a spare of such items.

Shopping by phone and the Internet

You may choose to shop online. Many stores and supermarkets offer an online service, accessible not just via your computer but via mobile phones as well. Without stirring from your chair, you can buy goods and services, and arrange to have shopping delivered. The advantages of online shopping are balanced by a few disadvantages. There will probably be delivery charges, and delivery times might not be flexible, but these aspects need to be set against the time that you spend getting to the shops, trawling round and queuing to pay (see Exercise 4.3 on p. 46).

Use your phone and the Internet to check the availability and prices of items. This could save you those wasted trips to buy goods that are no longer available or the last one of which has just been sold.

Exercise 4.3: Shopping online

Weigh up the pros and cons of doing your supermarket or other shopping online.

Name of shop   *Good things about its service*   *Things I don't like about its service*

1 _____

2 _____

3 _____

4 _____

Get someone else to do the boring bits

You might be able to delegate a family member to buy the routine household goods and toiletries (or to be there to take delivery of items). Another solution might be to pay a local teenager to do this chore. Sylvie operates this system. She enjoys some aspects of food shopping, like selecting fruit, vegetables, cheese, coffee, and finding bakeries which sell different types of bread, but hates buying in the tins and packets and the boring everyday stuff. Every month, in return for payment, her neighbour's son drives to the supermarket for her. Using the list that she draws up, he gets in a supply of the basics she needs. Dividing the tasks in this way gives Sylvie time to savour the kind of shopping that she enjoys.

Always have a list

You really will forget things if you don't make a list. Keep your list somewhere visible and easy to find at home where you and other members of the household can jot down items that need replacing. You could have a wipe-clean board for this, and use this record as the basis of your shopping list.

For food shopping, you will save time if you have in mind at least a rough plan for meals. Consult the list of what needs to be bought and look at your planner and diary as well. Knowing if people are going to be out, home late, or dashing in for a quick bite before rushing out again helps you to plan.

You will also save time by making a master list of basic items that you buy regularly. Keep it in a plastic folder. This means that you don't have to write a list over and over again, just add items when they are needed.

Arrange your shopping list

If you usually shop in the same supermarket, try arranging the items on your shopping list in the order in which they are placed in the store. Close your eyes and visualize yourself walking through the aisles. You could probably put most items in their aisle order right now, but in any case, if you decide to operate this system, one more visit to the shop and you will be able to do it. Once you get this system working it speeds up the shopping process remarkably.

If you have a variety of things to buy in different places, make a shopping list that groups together the items that you will buy in the same shop. That way your eye won't light on 'shampoo' as you go into the post office, and you will save time not going backwards and forwards between shops. If you are shopping in a familiar place arrange your groups of items in the order of the shops you will visit, so that you can streamline your route. Factor in a nice cafe and you can use the time that you save to have a cup of coffee.

Choose less crowded times

Sometimes the only choice we have is to squeeze shopping into a lunch hour or a Saturday afternoon. The time-saving choice is to avoid times when everyone else is shopping too. When it is possible to do so, take advantage of periods when shops are less crowded. You might need to do a bit of research to find out when your favourite supermarket is least busy, but if you can identify and use such a period you will save time and hassle.

Use your notebook

In the notebook that you keep with you, or on a piece of paper tucked into your purse, store information such as clothes sizes for you and your family, and other useful measurements and dimensions. You will find that this practice is handy when there is an item that you have not gone out specifically to purchase, but are vaguely thinking about buying or replacing. The chances are that you will see just the rug for the spare room, or come across an amazing special offer on school uniform items, when it is the last thing on your mind. If you can check essentials such as sizes there and then you will save having to make another visit because you haven't got the relevant information on you.

Shopping for clothes

Take with you your notes of which shops have the items you are looking for – you have jotted down these details, haven't you? If you are looking for something to go with a particular item of clothing, wear the item or take it with you.

Wear clothes that are easy to put on and take off. Struggling in and out of difficult-to-fasten garments and tricky layers of clothing can double the time that you spend in changing rooms. It also makes you so bad-tempered that you abandon the trip and have to do it all over again another time. Don't wear jewellery that is likely to get tangled up in your clothes.

Choose garments that you can take care of easily. Clothes that need to be regularly dry cleaned or require special attention eat into your time.

Buy two. Especially if it has taken you a long time to track down the perfect top or trousers, it's a good idea to buy two garments, even two in the same colour if you really love it. Odds are that you will never be able to find exactly or even nearly the same thing again.

Use a personal shopper – they are not just for celebrities and the rich. Many stores offer this service (sometimes for a small charge) and you will save loads of time. The shopper brings items that you have chosen or ones that, after discussion, he or she thinks will suit your budget and your taste. You have to get undressed once, then stay put in the dressing room as different garments are brought to you and wrong-size items replaced.

Buy gifts the time-saving way

We all know someone who does her Christmas and birthdays shopping in the January sales. We might secretly admire her and wish that we too could be so organized – but we just know that when the time came around we would forget where we had put all those carefully chosen gifts. However, it is worth adopting her strategy, because, depending on how many presents you buy and cards you send over the course of a year, you can save literally whole days by being prepared.

A wasted shopping trip

Gina is choosing a birthday present for Laura. She has in mind a silver chain and pendant that she spotted in the window of one of Laura's favourite shops, but Laura has said recently how much she likes those fringed scarves that everyone is wearing. So Gina thinks that she will just have a quick look round to see if she can find one in Laura's colours. She sees one in the department store, but it's a very expensive designer brand, so she has a trawl through town to find one that is very similar only cheaper. When she has no success, she goes back to the first shop, only to find that they have just sold the last pendant.

Gina loses out all round. She did not enjoy shopping for the birthday present, because she had left it until the last minute and felt under pressure, and the trip did not have a successful outcome. Gina feels that she has thrown away a couple of hours which she could have put to good use. What makes it worse is that a couple of months ago she spotted a little bag that she knew Laura would love, but thought, 'It's not her birthday for ages yet, so I'll get it nearer the time.' Of course, the moment passed and was gone for ever.

Buying appropriate gifts when you see them is a great time-saver. Although it is unlikely that you can do this for everyone on your list, you will be able to deal with a surprising number of obligations in this way. Presents for family and friends, work colleagues, children's teachers, party favours, little thank-you gifts, items of clothing, jewellery and accessories that you know someone will like – when it catches your eye and you think it will be suitable, buy it and put it in a designated place. Having a little store of gifts that make good last-minute presents really pays off. It means you will never have to spend two hours looking round for something suitable for your child's playgroup assistant who you have just discovered is leaving the next day.

Do the same with cards for birthdays and other occasions. Keep a varied selection in stock and you will always be able to send an appropriate greeting without having to make a special trip to buy a card.

Keep wrapping paper, sellotape and scissors in the same place as you store the presents, and the process of preparing gifts will run quickly and smoothly. You could even wrap presents as you buy them (attach a label saying what is inside). This will only take a few minutes and will save you precious time later on.

Make a note and keep a list of what you have bought. Do something nice with the time that you have saved.

Take the easiest option

When people make it easy for you, seize the opportunity. Unless you really want to spend time looking for, say, the perfect wedding present for a couple, choose an item from their list and order it by phone or online. Alternatively, send a gift voucher or money.

You could do the same for Christmas and birthday presents – just ask people what they want. If you feel that this mode of present-giving is impersonal, and you would much rather choose an item for each individual on your list, think about what part of your 'big picture' your preference supports. If it is to enhance relationships by making the gifts personal and meaningful, could you strike a personal note in another way, for example in the inscription that accompanies money or vouchers?

However, if you positively enjoy choosing presents, and take pleasure in gift-wrapping and creating lovely presentations, take the time to do this, at least for the people who matter. Expressing your creativity and personality and doing something you are good at and enjoy is a great use of time.

The following are presents that are quick to order and have delivered, by phone or online:

> Subscriptions to magazines
> Flowers and plants
> Gift certificates – book and music stores, department stores, beauty treatments
> 'Red letter day' vouchers
> Film or theatre vouchers
> Vouchers for services – car valet, professional house-cleaning, a life coaching session, a wardrobe makeover
> Memberships – National Trust, English Heritage, art galleries and museums

How to stop being late

Being late is a habit. How often do we say of someone, 'Oh, she's always late', or 'She's late – that's just like her'. If you are always running behind, stop and ask yourself why this is. It could be that you get some emotional gratification from being late, such as:

Enjoying the last-minute rush and panic.
Liking the way people look relieved or pleased to see you when
   you finally turn up.
Feeling justified in feeling aggrieved if people are annoyed when
   you finally turn up.
Add your own ideas:

If this is you, try to find some other way of getting these particular
needs met. If the buzz of preparation is important to you, start your
preparations earlier. Your adrenalin doesn't know what time it is,
and will flow as you anticipate and get worked up for departure. For
maximum effect, try pretending that you are running late.

If you find that you have time to spare, reward yourself by doing
something with an inbuilt excitement factor: play some music that
gets you going, or take a quick walk. Set your phone or watch to
warn you when time's up.

Tell yourself that people are even more pleased to see you when
you are on time. Anyway, they may have been only pretending not
to be annoyed.

With this new habit of being on time you will not need any defensive
strategies to help you cope with other people's annoyance. You will be
much more in control of your time and of yourself.

It could be that you have built-in ways of behaving that result in
your being late, such as:

Putting off the moment of leaving, stopping to do just one
   more thing.
Underestimating the time it will take you to get ready and get
   there.
Add your own ideas:

If this is you, try some of these strategies. Set a realistic departure time. Work backwards from the time that you are expected, factor in and allow time for everything that you have to do, and add half an hour as buffer time. Think in advance about the last-minute things that you usually do to delay departure. If they really need to be done, slot them in earlier. If they are merely delaying devices, put them out of your head and focus on your time of departure.

Reward yourself for being on time.

Some final time management tips

Make time-light lifestyle choices

It is possible that you can cut down on housekeeping time by making your home easy to maintain. Choose carpets and furnishings in fabrics that don't show up every mark. Don't have lots of ornaments and knick-knacks that need dusting.

If your garden is heavy on maintenance and you don't want to spend much time on it, or pay someone else to look after it, consider paving over some areas and having plants in pots. Choose plants that flourish throughout the year. Look for the words 'perennial' and 'hardy' on the labels.

However, if you enjoy doing the garden or caring for your home, find the time for it by cutting down on something else.

Set time limits

If you find that coffee meetings and lunch appointments run away with you, state the timescale that you are thinking of when you make the arrangement. You can do this pleasantly with friends: 'So that's lunch in the café on the fourth floor, one o'clock until two-thirty, say?' This is a good way of offering your limit and finding out what the other person has in mind.

Take time to enjoy

Remember that quickest isn't always best. Time management isn't about racing through life at top speed, it is about making choices that support your needs and goals. Sometimes the simple act of browsing through a shop or store can be an enjoyable and even productive way to spend time, because you come across items that you find interesting and useful, you get ideas and spark your creativity, you experience moments of pleasure. For example, buying books online is quick and easy. Going into a bookshop takes longer, but you may well unexpectedly discover titles that you would not have found otherwise. Subscribing to magazines and journals and having them delivered is a great time-saver, but actually browsing through a magazine rack can keep you in touch with new ideas and stimulate your interest.

Don't think that you have to fill every moment with activity. When you feel overloaded, or even when you don't, just retreat, mentally and physically. Take the time just to be – don't even consciously relax, or meditate. Just slow down and let yourself drift. It will replenish you, clear your mind, and help you to gain balance and perspective for making choices about how you want to spend your time.

5

Skills to help you make the best use of your time

Saying no

One of the ways in which we become overloaded is by taking too much on, and one reason we take too much on is that we find it hard to say no. Not being able to refuse a request, and always being ready to do what someone asks, means that we waste time and lose our grip on our own goals and priorities. Just this one skill, the ability to say no nicely and appropriately, could save masses of time and make your life much easier.

There are many occasions when we would like to say no to something, but make the choice to say yes. If you are happy that your choice is the right decision, then the best thing to do is to make some adjustments in other areas of your life so that you can fulfil this commitment.

Jennifer decides to say yes
Jennifer babysits for her young grandchildren once a week. It does not really suit her to do this on the designated evening, but it is the only time that her son and his wife can make the time to go out together. Saying no to the request would give Jennifer back her evening, but she thinks that in this instance the benefits of the arrangement outweigh the disadvantages to her.

On other occasions, we don't actually make the choice to agree, we just can't bring ourselves to say no (see Exercise 5.1).

Josie can't say no
Josie always drops what she is doing to help someone who asks. She does not always want to do this, but feels that she cannot refuse. At work she is always ready to lend a hand, for instance when a colleague can't find a particular file, or needs some help with a last-minute rush job. In her personal life, she accommodates requests for lifts and runs small errands for family members, even on those occasions when she thinks that the

request is unreasonable. The result of this habit is that Josie sometimes does not have time for her own work, and cannot plan her own activities.

Exercise 5.1: Losing time through saying yes to everything

Think about situations in which your reluctance or inability to say no to a request means that you spend your time in ways that you do not want to.

What I should say no to   *How much time I lose through saying yes*

1 _____   _____

2 _____   _____

3 _____   _____

4 _____   _____

Why we find it difficult to say no

We find ourselves agreeing to things against our will and against our better judgement for a number of reasons:

We want to be liked.
We want to be seen as co-operative.
We like the person who is asking.
We are scared of the person who is asking.
The other person might feel hurt if we say no.
Fear that we will damage our relationship with the other person.
Add your own ideas:

What you will gain from learning to say no

Most of our fears about the consequences of refusing a request are ill-founded and outweighed by the advantages of gaining more time and more control over your time. As soon as you stop saying yes to everything your load will lighten. For some of us, realizing and accepting that just because someone asks you to do something, it doesn't always mean that you have to do it, is a great break-through. By saying no to requests when it is appropriate to do so you will gain:

- *Self–esteem.* Once you realize that you have a right to refuse a request, and that you can say no gracefully and effectively, your self-confidence will rocket.
- *Respect from others.* Other people will appreciate that you value your time and you can make decisions about how to use it. You gain a reputation for being not only focused on the best use of your time, but open and fair as well.
- *The ability to be effective.* You can't be effective if you say yes to everything that comes your way. Knowing what to turn down and being able to do so helps you make the best use of your time.
- *More control of your life.* You can't control time, but you can take some control of yourself and your life. Exercising choices is a way of managing events rather than letting them manage you.
- *Above all – time.* If you can't say no, your time gets filled up with activities that are not your choice or your duty. Being selective about how you spend your time whenever possible gives you space to focus on what is important to you.

Hang on to the 'big picture'

One way to help you deal with saying no is to keep the big picture in mind. Focus on your overall aims and goals and ask yourself how saying no to this particular request will affect them. By saying that you will not be helping at the fund-raiser this year will you damage your big picture aim of being involved in the community? Does turning down an invitation to a lunch or a night out with your pals mean that you are not a good friend? Does refusing to look for your teenager's missing sports kit, which he has mislaid, scupper your goal of being a supportive mother? In most cases, saying no will not have an adverse effect. You probably know if the effect of refusing a request would be damaging or disastrous, in which case you will choose to agree to it, regardless of the conse-quences to yourself and your time.

How to say no

Ideally we want to say no and still:

- Have friends.
- Manage not to alienate our family.
- Keep our job.

There are different ways of saying no, depending on what kind of 'no' you mean. Sometimes we mean no, not now. Sometimes we mean no, not in that way, or no, not without help. There are occasions when you want to give a reason for your refusal, and there are occasions when you do not.

Some guidelines apply to all situations.

Take your time

Pause before you reply. Use little 'fillers' like 'Right', 'Okay, let's see', 'Oh, I see'. They mean nothing but give you a breathing space. While your mouth is uttering a phrase like this it is not uttering a 'yes' that you may later regret. Another way of slowing down is to take a deep breath and expel the air slowly. This buys you time and also helps you to remain calm so that you can give a considered response.

Make sure that you have understood the request

A good way of ascertaining some sense of the time commitment involved is to repeat what has been asked: 'So what you want is for me to drive you over to Mira's house, wait while you pick up your things, then drive you back across town to your play rehearsal', 'You want to know if I will ask local firms for raffle donations', 'You need me to help you to set up the database'.

Get all the details

You need to know exactly what is involved before you decide. If necessary, pin down vague requests such as, 'Can you help me out with this just until I sort the house out/Jamie gets settled at school/ we appoint someone permanent', etc. Get a precise timescale, so that you know what is involved. 'Just for now' or 'It'll only be for a few weeks' can turn into time-eating monsters.

Ask for thinking time. If you need time to consider the request, say so. A nice way to do this is to reflect the person's need, and if you want to, give your response:

'I can see that you have got a lot on at the moment, and I
would like to help you. I do need to think this one through,
though. I'll get back to you ...'

'Thanks for asking me to join the working group. It sounds like
a fascinating project. I'll mull it over and let you know ...'

Always let someone know when you will reply, and in what form:

'I'll email you by the end of the day.'

'I'll phone you before Friday.'

Sasha's charity fun run

When Sasha is asked to help with marshalling for the charity fun run, she says
yes straight away. She is free on the day, and would like to help. When she
discovers that she will have to attend a couple of meetings and an evening
first aid course, she wishes that she had said no to this particular request,
which has come at a time when she has several other commitments.

Don't take too much time

Don't ask for time just as a stalling measure. If you know that you
want to say no, it is always best to get it over and done with quickly
and gracefully. Don't get the other person's hopes up. Use phrases
such as:

'I'm very committed at the moment. I will think about it, and
phone you this afternoon.'

'Thanks for asking me. I'll give it some thought and let you know
by the end of the week, but I have to say it's not quite my thing.'

'I can see that you're stuck, but I'm afraid that I can't help at
the moment.'

'I know you want a lift to Sandi's, but I'm not going out again.'

When appropriate, say what you are willing to do

'I'm not willing to drive your over to Sandi's tonight, but I'll
take you to the ice rink on Saturday.'

'I'm going to say no to running a stall at the fair, but I'm happy
to sell raffle tickets.'

'I'm not able to work late tonight, but I could do an extra hour
on Tuesday or Thursday.'

When you offer an alternative, however, just be careful that you don't
get talked into doing both things.

Lead the other person to back off

This strategy takes a bit of effort, but is a helpful way of leading some-one into the habit of thinking about requests before making them. What you do is discourage people from automatically asking you, and encourage them to work situations through for themselves or find their own solutions. You need to invest a certain amount of time in this, but in the end it will be a great saver of your time and theirs.

Kerry writes her emails

Kerry is using her home computer to write some personal emails. When her son says, 'I need to use the computer now. There's stuff I have to look up for school', instead of sighing and logging off, then feeling disgruntled all evening, she says, 'Well, as you can see, I'm using the computer now and will be for the next half-hour. What homework or other activity could you do for half an hour?'

She sticks to her guns, ignores the complaints of 'Nothing!' and her son does find something else to do. If necessary, she is ready to talk him through some options: What exactly is the information he needs? When exactly is it needed by? Is there any other way he could get it?

Of course, this process would take time, but it gets across valuable messages about planning and using one's own and other people's time.

Suggest a different time-frame

'Being realistic, I'm unlikely to manage it by Tuesday, but I could certainly get it done by Thursday.'

Involve other people

'Can you help me here? Raj wants me to help out on the desk, but I'm in the middle of doing this survey for Cris. Any ideas how we can sort it out?'

'Here's the situation. I've got half an hour before I leave for yoga. Naomi wants me to help with her project, and James wants a hand filling out his job application. Why don't the two of you sort it out and let me know what you come up with?'

What not to say

Avoid certain phrases. Saying something like 'I can't, I'm too busy', can be like a red rag to a bull. Aren't we all 'busy'? A similar one to avoid is 'I haven't got time'. The person asking knows that you have got time, just as much time as anybody else, but that you are choosing to spend your time differently, so you are just making a feeble excuse, or that you cannot see how to arrange your schedule to make time to meet this particular request. If it is the latter situation, people are very happy to help you make suitable arrangements to free up time for you to do what they want.

Try not to say 'maybe' or 'perhaps' when you have already decided that you will say no.

Be careful with the types of question when you are asking for more information. As we have seen, it is a very good idea to find out all you need to know before committing yourself, but asking lots of questions just to put off the moment of saying no is annoying to the other person – and a time-waster!

Remember that if you sound positive and helpful your 'no' will be accepted and people will respect your honesty and your pleasant directness.

Exercise 5.2: Putting saying no into practice

Keep track of the occasions that you refuse a request which you would previously have agreed to. Work out how much time you have saved.

What I said no to *How much time I gained*

1

2

3

4

5

6

7

8

9

10

How to deal with interruptions

Sometimes interruptions are welcome breaks from what you are doing, and at other times they constitute an annoying intrusion.

Interruptions are particularly irritating when they break the flow of your activity, so that you not only lose time dealing with them, but it takes you a while to get back into the swing of what you were doing (see Exercise 5.3).

The reasons we allow ourselves to be interrupted constantly are the same kinds of reasons that make us say yes to everything. We think that unless we accept the interruption we will be seen as unfriendly and unco-operative. Perhaps we are flattered that people want to ask us things, to pick our brains. We like to be liked and to know that others enjoy being with us. However, if you have a respect for time, not allowing interruption and not interrupting people yourself is also a way of showing self-respect and respect for others.

Exercise 5.3: What interrupts you?

Think about a typical day or week, and chart what kinds of interruptions break into your time.

	Who interrupts me	What they want	Why they ask me
1			
2			
3			
4			
5			

How to challenge interruptions

Rather than respond to every interruption, ask yourself some questions to determine if it is necessary to give the matter your immediate attention. These could include:

What will happen if I do not help this person right now?
What will happen if I do not answer the phone right now?
What will happen if I do not check my emails right now?
What will happen if I do not stop and talk to Marcie?
What will happen if I do not stop what I am doing to listen to Jerry's story about the strange customer?

Having thought through some possible consequences, you can decide how to respond to the interruption (see Exercise 5.4). You can get used to applying this technique very quickly.

Exercise 5.4: How important is the interruption?

	Situation	Nature of interruption	Consequences of not accepting it	Decision
1	_____	_____	_____	_____
2	_____	_____	_____	_____
3	_____	_____	_____	_____
4	_____	_____	_____	_____
5	_____	_____	_____	_____
6	_____	_____	_____	_____

Once you have identified situations in which it is not appropriate to let yourself be interrupted, you need some strategies to help you to minimize interruptions and keep them at bay.

Dealing with drop-in visitors

When people drop in on you at home or call by your work station when you are in the middle of something you really don't want to put on hold, don't just assume that there's nothing you can do about it. If you are happy to give your attention to the interruption, try making it clear that while you acknowledge someone's claim on your time, you are putting a limit on how much of it you can give. Instead of saying, 'Hello, Richard!' try 'Hello Richard, how can I help you?' or 'Hello Richard, what can I do for you?' These expressions make it clear that you have time only for a purposeful exchange.

If you feel that this sounds unfriendly, you can soften the phrase by saying something like, 'Hello, Richard. Listen, I've only got a few minutes right now', or 'This isn't a good time for me. Can I catch up with you later?'

When the person immediately starts talking, break in quickly with something like, 'I'd love to hear more about that. I only have five minutes at the moment, though.' If someone asks you if you've 'got a minute', be quite precise about how much time you have. Saying 'I have got ten minutes at the moment. Will that be enough?' is helpful to you and to the other person.

It is best to make your position clear right away. If you let someone launch into whatever is on their mind, it is much more difficult to cut them off. If you are still worried about sounding cold, think about how other people may feel when they realize that they have interrupted you and you have been waiting for them to finish and leave, and try to interrupt them gently.

If you want a conversation to be short, don't let the other person become too comfortable. Stand up when someone comes towards you; don't invite them to sit down. Don't get drawn into small talk. When your visitor starts to chat, acknowledge briefly what has been said, then direct the conversation back to the point: 'That does sound fun. About the presentation – is there anything else you need to know?'

How to end conversations and meetings

There may be some conversations and encounters that you never want to end, but others drag on long past the point where they are useful or enjoyable. Whether you are speaking in person or on the phone, there are phrases you can put to use to bring it to a close. A good strategy is to signal that you are coming to the end of a conversation by using phrases such as:

> 'Before we hang up ...'
> 'Just one last thing ...'
> 'Before I let you get on with your shopping ...'
> 'I'll let you get back to ...'

If you use the past tense, you send a message that the conversation is over:

> 'I've enjoyed talking to you.'
> 'This has been really useful.'

You can also give visual signals that time is up by looking at your watch, gathering together papers or personal items, and picking up your bag.

Asking for what you want

The ability to make requests clearly and assertively is essential if you are to gain and maintain control of your time. Work on your assertion skills and get yourself into the right frame of mind to make your request. Remind yourself that it is all right for you to ask, that you are being proactive and taking responsibility for getting tasks done. You are not begging for a favour, you are making a suggestion that will help you to use your time more productively.

People respond positively to positive language and positive suggestions, so spend a little time preparing your approach. Don't put yourself down, or whinge and complain, but describe the situation, and show what will be gained from your suggestion. Show that you are prepared to discuss and negotiate.

Dawn's workload

Dawn's workload has gradually increased, and she has not been given any extra time to deal with the new tasks. She would like to negotiate a change, but feels that she cannot approach her line manager about this in case she is seen to be incompetent or unable to cope.

Dawn should not say anything like: 'I didn't say anything at first, but I've been really overloaded with all this extra work, and I've been busting a gut trying to get everything done.'

Instead she could say: 'I've been thinking about ways of dealing with the increased workload. What do you think about asking Jon to take on the ordering? That would give me more time to make a good job of the rest.'

Trudy and the school run

Trudy needs to ask another mother about sharing the school run. She begins by describing the situation: 'I notice that we both drive to school from the same part of town.' Then she puts the request in terms that include the other person: 'What do you think about sharing the run? If you like the idea, we could work out a system that suits us both.'

Speedy decision-making – making good and quick choices

Making decisions is hard. We worry that we will get it wrong, we worry that even if we get it right we won't be able to deal with the changes or the unforeseeable circumstances that follow making a choice. Not only can we become paralysed with indecision, we can waste hours of valuable time agonizing over choices, and lose our sense of proportion, spending ages dithering over issues that are not all that important. Sometimes we feel that we cannot come to a conclusion until we have explored every single option and gathered every possible piece of information that might be useful.

Check your own attitude to decision-making

- Do you spend a long time making up your mind about even trivial matters?
- Once you have made a decision, do you worry about whether it is the right one?
- Do you let other people decide things for you?
- Do you put off making a decision because it will involve changing something that you are used to?
- Does worrying about getting it wrong prevent you from making a decision?
- Have you ever missed out on something because you weren't able to make a decision?

If you answered yes to several of these questions, it is probable that you find it difficult to deal with choices, and that you put off having to come to a decision, maybe hoping that the issue will go away or resolve itself. However, if you keep a clear head and bear in mind your major goals and priorities, even major decisions can be made quite quickly.

Top time-saving tip for decision-making: always bear in mind the outcome that you want.

How to make decisions

Follow a decision-making process (see Exercise 5.5, p. 68). Use the following system for situations that you want to change, and for making important, life-affecting decisions.

1 Weigh up the pros and cons

Sometimes tricky problems can be resolved with a run-down of the pros and cons involved. Remember Kate's dilemma about the amount of time she spends taking her children to different activities? She changed her attitude to the situation by considering the big picture, and supported the process of change by asking herself what are the advantages and disadvantages of the present situation. This is her list of pros and cons:

What is lost and what is gained through this use of time?
Gains
Kids do activities they enjoy.
This is good for their development and supports what I want for
  them.
Losses
I have no time in the week for anything else.
My personal life and my relationships are suffering as a result.
I feel guilty for resenting the time I spend being a taxi service.
The kids are not learning about making choices.
What outcome do I want?
The kids to do some activities they enjoy and I have more time.

2 Generate solutions

Now Kate is free to move on to make some decisions about how
to change the situation. A good way to get ideas is to take a large
sheet of paper and jot down all the possible ways of achieving the
desired outcome. Don't stop and think 'Yes, but', or 'That won't
work because …' Just fill the sheet with as many ideas as you can
think of. Kate's sheet looks like this:

Children to choose one activity per term.
Can do more than one activity but must be on same night so
  that only one evening is taken up.
Find someone else doing activity and share driving – alternate
  weeks or one to pick up and one to drop off.
Cost of taxi? If shared?
Any classes within walking distance?
Public transport?
No weekday activities during termtime but sign up for intensive
  courses during school holidays.
Ask children for their suggestions and solutions.

3 Select one or two solutions

This process opens up ideas, and helps Kate to see that there is in
fact more than one way of solving her problem.

4 Engage with your emotions

Once you have identified a solution that makes sense and will
work, test your emotional reaction. Are you or can you become
comfortable with the course of action you have chosen? If you

find that negative feelings are aroused, think about the source of those feelings and examine the ideas and beliefs that create them. Are you hanging on to old ideas and attitudes about what you should and shouldn't do? Do you have some ingrained beliefs about how you should behave as a mother, or a friend, that make it hard for you to change the way that you use your time?

When a logical solution points you in one direction and your heart points you in another, trust your instincts. Check them out, as we have discussed – don't dismiss them. The right decision isn't always the one that makes sense on paper.

5 Put it into action

Write down the next step you will take to get your plan going.

Just do it

Sometimes you just need to make a decision. Most of the choices we have to make aren't matters of life and death, and are not worth spending precious time on.

Limit your options

Too many choices
Valerie wants to decorate the spare bedroom and just cannot decide on a style and colour scheme. She spends ages flipping through magazines and colour charts, asking her friends and visiting DIY stores to get samples, and at the same time feels frustrated because the room really needs doing and nothing is happening.

Teresa's daughter wants a dress for the end of year prom. Together they have spent ages trawling the Internet and the shops. There are one or two strong possibilities, but the thought that the perfect dress is out there somewhere prolongs the time-consuming search.

Having too many choices makes decision-making difficult and time-consuming. Try narrowing down your options and imagining that the others don't exist. Having done some groundwork, Valerie could just opt for a particular colour range and put the others out of her mind. Or she could decide to make her choices from one chosen outlet or one book of samples. Once the room is attractively decorated, she is unlikely to dwell on the choices she rejected.

Exercise 5.5: Using a decision-making process

Use this process on one of the problems facing you at the moment.
Problem:_____

_____

Good things about the present situation: _____

_____

Negative things about the present situation: _____

_____

The outcome that I want: _____

_____

All the things that could be done to improve the situation: _____

_____

_____

_____

Three solutions:
1 _____
2 _____
3 _____

How I feel about these solutions: _____

_____

_____

_____

Action plan:

Step 1   _____By when:_____
Step 2   _____By when:_____
Step 3   _____By when:_____

Teresa could choose a shopping area or a number of specified shops and decide that this is where the dress will be bought. After all, many purchases involve a degree of compromise, and even if the perfect dress is lurking somewhere, the chances of its being the perfect price, the perfect size and the perfect colour are probably slim, and what is more likely is that after hours and hours of tracking down this garment her daughter will change her mind ...

Sleep on it

Let your subconscious mind do the work while you are asleep. Sometimes we wake up knowing just what we need to do, with the solution staring us in the face. A variation on this is putting something out of your mind and becoming absorbed in another activity. When you think again about the problem, it can appear with a new clarity.

Do one thing rather than let it drift on

Delay often makes things worse. When something is on your mind and you can't decide what to do, do just one thing that will move the situation on a little bit.

Don't dwell on the alternatives

Once you have made up your mind, put your decision into action and don't waste time wondering if you have done the right thing. Instead, get on with making your decision work.

Speed reading

The ability to take in written information quickly and accurately will save you lots of time. This skill can be applied when you need to take in the essence of the material and to assimilate what is important and relevant to you. Use speed reading for documents, reports, books – any kind of document or package of information that you do not wish to linger over for ages. You will find this skill particularly useful in coping with a workload that involves reading through lots of material.

Before you go on, remember that we are not discussing the kinds of books, magazines and periodicals that you choose to read for pleasure and enjoyment. These are to be savoured and relished at leisure.

Speed reading is suitable for material and information that you need to take in for a specific purpose. You can use it for:

Work-related reports and documents.
Information about children's education – instructions about
    procedures, fees, grants, applications.
Recipes.
Instruction manuals.
Travel timetables and information.

Books you read for study purposes – course books, text books.
Books and articles you want to get a flavour of without actually
reading every word (very useful for reading group cheats).
Reading information on the Internet.

Know the purpose of your reading. Decide what you need to get out of the material. You might be looking for specific information, checking out if there is anything of interest to you, or following a set of instructions.

When you are looking for information, you do not need to read every word of the text. Instead, use these speed reading techniques.

Skimming

When you skim material you do not actually read it – you look over it to get a general idea of what it is about. This technique can help you to decide if you need to invest more time in reading the material carefully. Instead of starting at the beginning and ploughing through every word, look at aspects such as:

Chapter or section headings
Indexes
Information about the writer
Introductions
Conclusions
Random pages and passages to get a sense of what the material
is like

Scanning

Scanning helps you to locate a particular piece of information. When you look up a TV guide to find out if your favourite programme is on or when it begins, your eye travels over the listings as you look for the key word or phrase that you want. It's the technique you use when you look up a name in a phone book, or check food values on a product label.

Once you have scanned the material, you can decide if you need to pay it closer attention.

Helpful techniques for reading quickly and effectively

- Train your eyes to take in more at a glance. Instead of looking at individual words, look at phrases and chunks of text.

- Move your eye down the centre of the page rather than from left to right.
- Use a pointer to help you. Position it at the top of the page and bring it down through the middle or along the margin to guide your eyes through the text. You can use your finger for this, or a pencil.
- Jot down notes as you read, just odd phrases and key words that will remind you of important points.
- When you are skimming through something, mark pages or passages you might want to return to. Use bookmarks or little stick-ons for this.
- When you come across something in a newspaper that you want to cut out later, make a tear at the top of the page so that you can easily locate it.
- Try not to say the words out loud to yourself, or hear them in your head.
- Try not to look back over the bit that you have read.

Break the rules

If you are one of those people who have self-imposed rules about reading, stop and think if these rules make for a productive or wasteful use of your time.

'I have to finish a book once I start it.' Who says that you have to? There is no great book monitor in the sky checking up on you. If you are not finding something enjoyable or useful, ditch it and move on to something else.

'I have to read every word.' As we have seen, you do not need to take in every detail. It all depends what you are reading for. Sometimes it is a very good idea to skip pages or passages.

Tune into your body clock

Your energy level affects your productivity. You may have noticed how at certain times of the day you whip through tasks with ease, whereas at other times the same tasks take for ever. Getting to know your personal body clock will help you to match activities to your moods and energy curve.

Early birds and night owls

Megan snaps into full alertness the moment she wakes up. She gets up ahead of everyone else in the household and uses the early morning hours very productively. By the middle of the afternoon she is flagging and needs a boost or a pick-me-up of some kind, and she likes an easy evening followed by an early night. For example, Megan does her most effective studying in the early morning, and would always choose to set the alarm and get up early rather than try to work on into the late evening.

Marsha is the opposite. It takes her ages to come round from sleep, and she is sluggish for most of the morning. By the afternoon she is buzzing and ready for anything, and is very happy to keep going through the evening. Marsha's most effective studying takes place later in the day, and her preference has always been to carry on into the evening to get something finished, than to have a morning lie-in.

Our body clocks influence our performance levels and our ability to concentrate – and they cannot be changed. Nothing can turn a night person into a morning person or vice versa. However, most of us do not experience extreme swings over the course of a day, but come somewhere between Megan and Marsha. Many of us pick up as the day goes on, then have a little dip, followed by a gentle recovery to take us into the evening.

As a quick check on your energy levels, think about the time of day at which you find it easiest to study and concentrate. This will give you a rough idea of how you function. Another check is to monitor your levels at the weekend or on the days when you don't work. How does your energy fluctuate when you are on holiday? You may find that you are up and ready for anything first thing in the morning as usual, even though you are keeping late hours. Exercise 5.6 shows a way of identifying your peaks and troughs more closely.

Matching activities to your energy levels

Once you are familiar with the pattern of your body clock try to adapt to your own rhythm and as far as you can match your different activities to your varying energy levels. Taking on a difficult task when you are feeling a bit tired and swimmy isn't a good idea – you won't give it your best shot, and the time that you spend on it will probably be wasted as you may well have to do it all over again. In the same way, don't waste your buzziest period on activities that don't require a lot of you. If you are full of energy at the beginning of the day, don't waste it by trawling through emails and making undemanding phone calls. If you feel sharp in the middle of the evening, capitalize

Exercise 5.6: Identify your body rhythms

Track your concentration levels over the course of a day. After each hour, give yourself a rating between 1 and 10, where 1 represents total lack of alertness and an inability to concentrate, and 10 represents your optimum level of concentration and alertness.

Time	Rating
6.00	1 2 3 4 5 6 7 8 9 10
7.00	1 2 3 4 5 6 7 8 9 10
8.00	1 2 3 4 5 6 7 8 9 10
9.00	1 2 3 4 5 6 7 8 9 10
10.00	1 2 3 4 5 6 7 8 9 10
11.00	1 2 3 4 5 6 7 8 9 10
12.00	1 2 3 4 5 6 7 8 9 10
13.00	1 2 3 4 5 6 7 8 9 10
14.00	1 2 3 4 5 6 7 8 9 10
15.00	1 2 3 4 5 6 7 8 9 10
16.00	1 2 3 4 5 6 7 8 9 10
17.00	1 2 3 4 5 6 7 8 9 10
18.00	1 2 3 4 5 6 7 8 9 10
19.00	1 2 3 4 5 6 7 8 9 10
20.00	1 2 3 4 5 6 7 8 9 10
21.00	1 2 3 4 5 6 7 8 9 10
22.00	1 2 3 4 5 6 7 8 9 10
23.00	1 2 3 4 5 6 7 8 9 10
24.00	1 2 3 4 5 6 7 8 9 10

Make a record of your pattern

Times when I am most alert: _____

Times when I am least alert: _____

Times when I flag just a bit: _____

on it by finding a way of doing just one or two tasks that require energy (see Exercise 5.7, p. 74).

You might need to break some ingrained habits to make this work. Tell yourself that it is perfectly acceptable, in fact it is a very good idea (if possible), to have a quick nap in the afternoon, early evening, or whenever it is that your energy dips. If it works for you to blitz the bathroom or fill in your passport application form at a time of the day that might seem odd to others, that's fine.

You will have your own preferences, but consider adapting them in the light of research that has identified the best time of day for certain activities.

Activities best done in the morning

Exercise

Research shows that morning exercise has a greater feel-good factor and makes you feel that you have exerted yourself more than in exercise taken at other times of the day.

Brain work and memorizing: facts, figures, speeches, presentations

Our short-term memory is 15 per cent more efficient in the morning, and our brains are at their sharpest before midday. But don't worry, you haven't missed your opportunity if you can't get to that tough assignment until after lunch, because we get a second surge of brain power in the mid-afternoon. Our long-term memory functions at its best at this time.

Exercise 5.7: Match your regular activities to your energy levels

Things to do when I am at my lowest ebb: _____

_____

Things to do when I am most alert and sharp: _____

_____

Things to do when I am dipping just a little: _____

_____

When you need to be alert

Often you just need to do things, no matter what you feel like. Pick-me-ups that work include:

- *A short rest*. The siesta has a lot to recommend it. If you can close your eyes for a few minutes or even have a short nap you will recharge your batteries and be ready to carry on.
- *Change what you are doing*. Sometimes the simple act of doing something different can spark your energy levels.
- *Get some fresh air*. A quick walk up the road, round the block or from building to building can help to give you the necessary boost.

- *Listen to some rousing and invigorating music.*
- *Have an energy-giving drink.* A strong coffee might be just what you need.
- *Eat something to boost your energy.* The best idea is to eat sustaining, energy-boosting food anyway, so that your dips aren't ever that bad. If you get into the habit of eating food that releases energy slowly, like porridge and bananas and wholemeal bread, you will prevent severe swings in energy levels. Quick-fix sugary foods give you a boost but their effect is short-lived and they are a bad health choice. At the same time, a piece of chocolate won't kill you, and the feel-good effect could mean that you function more effectively.

How to make accurate time estimations

This simple skill can give you a measure of control over your time. Many of us underestimate the amount of time needed or spent on particular tasks. We say things like 'I'll be ready in two ticks/no time at all', phrases that show our desire to be ready quickly but which do not relate to the reality of the situation. Almost invariably the activities that follow the phrase 'I'll just ...' involve much more time than the phrase suggests. 'I'll just put on the washing'; 'I'll just make a quick phone call'; 'I'll just pop to the shops'; 'I'll just check my emails' – all these can take a variable amount of time, and usually longer than you suppose.

Work out exactly how long it takes you to get ready in the morning, and when you go out. You know your own routine; if you can't be precise, time yourself. It's really helpful to know that you need, say, half an hour before you are fit to face the world. This gives you a definite time period and helps you plan. Do the same with your evening bedtime routine. Knowing how much time you take in the bathroom, the time you need to prepare for the next day, or to vacuum the living room and so on is a great planning aid.

Once you know how long your routines take, you may be able to find ways of streamlining them without losing the quality of the result.

Dealing with paperwork

People used to, and perhaps still do, talk about the paperless office and paperless home, where all transactions take place and are stored on computers, enabling us to live in clutter-free zones, our desks, work surfaces and kitchen tables unsullied by piles of paper. The reality is likely to be very different. We have mail, bills, policies, records, reference materials, memos, bulletins, newsletters, circulars, reports, cards, invitations, all requiring some kind of attention. A common habit is to put everything in a pile to be dealt with later, then the piles grow and spread and dealing with them becomes a major task. It is worth getting into the habit of dealing with paperwork as it comes in rather than letting it all pile up and having a massive sort-out when it becomes too overwhelming.

The time-saving way to deal with paperwork is not to let it take too much of your attention. Give each piece just the amount of attention necessary to decide which category to put it in. A common piece of advice is that we should handle every piece of paper only once, but in practice this doesn't work very well – we may need a bit of time to think about how we are going to deal with something. What we can decide right away, however, is what kind of response the paper requires. Try this three-step time-saving way of dealing with paperwork.

Step 1: Decide what can be thrown away

And once you have decided, throw it away immediately. Try to get rid of as much of the actual paper as you can. Some pieces of paper require you to do something – pay a bill, answer a query, take a particular action, reply to an invitation. If an action is required, write down a reminder, on your list, in your notebook, or wherever you put such information. There is no need to keep the card or letter from your dentist or optician reminding you to make an appointment. Jot down a note to make the phone call, and bin the letter. If you receive details of a meeting, make a note of what you need and throw away the memo. When you receive change-of-address notification, write down the new address straight away and get rid of the card or letter. When there is a number or a reference that you need to keep, again, make a note of it and destroy the document.

There is loads you don't need to keep. Sometimes we hang on to, for example, old household bills 'just in case', without asking the question 'just in case what?' It's the same with old cheque book stubs, and bank statements. You might want to keep the most recent of these items, but really, do you want to spend even a minute of your time checking what your electricity bill was ten years ago?

Step 2: Decide what you need to keep

Some items you do need to hang on to – those that require a decision that you want to think about, or that contain information that you need to digest carefully, or if they are important reference documents that should be kept safe.

If items in this category require action at some point, jot down a reminder to yourself to deal with them at an appropriate time, e.g. 'Pay repair bill', 'Answer wedding invitation', 'Read article about home schooling'.

Step 3: Put the item in its designated place

Filing and storing

It is useful to have a filing system of some kind. You will save hours if you keep only the papers that you really need and know exactly where they are. There are some excellent books on decluttering and organizing your life which will help you to evolve a system that is just right for your needs (see Further reading). Here are a few suggestions that will make the process of handling paperwork smooth and speedy. Pick and choose ideas that you can put into practice.

Use what works for you – choose from boxes, sets of drawers, document folders or plastic envelopes. There is a wide range of stationery available to enable you to set up a system that does the job and is nice to use. You don't need office space as such in your home to keep on top of papers and documents.

Have a 'file' for each family member. In each one put that person's essential documentation and other relevant items.

Have a place to file everything that you want to keep. You might need sections in your system headed:

Household bills
Bank and finance
Emergency numbers
Services (names and numbers of plumbers, decorators, etc.)
Appliances (guarantees, repair history, etc.)
Recipes

Items to be read (articles you've clipped from newspapers and
magazines before throwing them away)
Holidays and travelling
Takeaways and restaurants
Entertainment (details of cinemas, theatres, shows)
Contact numbers for children's friends and families

Make sure that you and all appropriate others know how the system
is organized.

Have a 'bring-forward' file. Use a concertina file, or anything
with sections that can be labelled for every day or every week or
month. What you do is file papers in the section with the relevant
date, and every evening empty the next day's pocket. So if you have
a bill that needs to be paid in two weeks' time, you put the bill in
that day's slot. When you come to empty that day's pocket, there it
is, ready for you to deal with.

Prune paper regularly

Even the most well-organized of us find that paper mounts up behind
our backs. Set aside a time every week, or month, whatever suits you,
to go through your files and weed out material that is out of date and
no longer needed. Not only will this save you time in that you will be
able to find what you want quickly, it will also remove distractions
that might make other tasks even longer, as you spend ten minutes
studying the take-away menu from the restaurant that has closed down
or reading the flyers for plays that you missed at the local theatre.

Top time-saving tip for keeping on top of paperwork

Never keep any piece of paper that might come in useful 'one day'.
The day will probably never come, or if it does, the information
will probably be out of date. Anyway, in the age of the information
highway, we can quickly find out most things that we need.

Labels

You may find it useful to get a label-maker. Labels make items easy
to see so they are less likely to get lost.

Cards

Have printed or make yourself some cards containing your personal
details, rather like business cards. Include your name, address,
phone numbers, email address and any other information that

may be useful. Giving out cards isn't just for business purposes. You will find them useful in all kinds of situations – ordering goods in shops, exchanging details with someone you have met, giving to the parents of your children's friends, and so on. They are particularly handy if your name is unusual or needs to be spelled out for people. You could even design a card that reflects your personality and that does not look like a business card.

Checklists

Devise your own checklists to help you get organized for regular or one-off events, such as:

> Going on holiday
> Christmas and other festivals
> Birthday celebrations
> Getting the children ready for the new school year
> Spring cleaning the house
> Doing the garden
> Children's sleepovers
> Weekend/night away
> *Add your own ideas:*

Draw up a prototype on the computer, then run off a fresh chart for each event. Your checklists could have space to write in what needs to be done and when it needs to be done by. Include a column to fill in who is going to do it – a handy delegation tool (see Exercise 5.8, p. 80). Pin the checklist up in a place where everyone can see it.

Lynne's summer holiday

Lynne starts to make a checklist for her summer holiday. She doesn't think about the order in which things will be done, she just writes down everything as she thinks of it. In the end she has a basic list that can be adapted when necessary.

Summer holiday

What	By when	By whom	Tick when done
Check passports			☐
Book kennels			☐
Get currency			☐
Buy swim stuff for Ali			☐
Book vaccines			☐
Ali to make own packing list			☐
Ian to make own packing list			☐
Book beauty salon appointment			☐
Buy sun creams			☐
Book taxi to airport			☐
Cancel papers			☐
Cancel milk			☐
Check Joan can water plants			☐
Leave key with Joan			☐
Turn off water/electricity			☐

Exercise 5.8: Make your own checklists

Choose three events for which you could use a checklist. Draw up the list for each one.

6

Sharing the load

Delegation

One way of sharing the load is to delegate, at work, at home, in your social life. Some people have a limited concept of delegating. They think of it just in a work context, as a mark of authority that entitles managers to pass down work to team members and junior staff. Of course, managers, good managers that is, do delegate work, but the concept is more wide-reaching. Delegation is all about sharing out the work so that more gets done, tasks are accomplished more easily and people's time is used most effectively. It is a skill that you can use at home to spread household tasks and activities, and a strategy that can be employed when organizing social events. It is a way of achieving what needs to be done more quickly and often with better results than if you did every single thing yourself. This one skill can free up time in every area of your life.

Yet this strategy, with all its advantages, is one that we are often reluctant to use. We find reasons and excuses to carry on doing too much ourselves, rather than let go and pass tasks on to other people (see Exercise 6.1, p. 82).

Margie does it all
Margie does practically everything around the house. She cooks, and clears the dishes, she gathers all the clothes for washing (she has tried to get the kids to put their clothes straight into the linen basket, but they never remember) and does the laundry as well as all the ironing. If she didn't push the vacuum round whenever she has a moment the house would be knee-deep in dust. Margie is the person everyone calls on when they can't find what they are looking for, as if she has extra powers to locate things. It's difficult keeping on top of all these tasks and doing her job as well, but she feels that she is the only one who can get the household to run smoothly.

Why we don't delegate

If your lists in Exercise 6.1 are long, it is likely that you have painted yourself into a corner. You do too much, and you have probably

Exercise 6.1: Are you indispensable?

In the home

I am the only one (or nearly the only one) who:

Knows where these things are kept

_____

_____

Knows how these things work

_____

_____

Does these things

_____

_____

Remembers to

_____

_____

Does these things properly

_____

_____

Outside the home

I am the only one (or nearly the only one) who:

Knows where these things are kept

_____

_____

Knows how these things work

_____

_____

Does these things

_____

_____

Remembers to

_____

_____

Does these things properly

_____

_____

found reasons like those below to justify this state of affairs. Some
of the reasons we give for not delegating include:

> I could do it more quickly myself.
> It would take too long to show someone else how to do this.
> No one will do it as well as I do.
> No one will do it in exactly the way I want it done.
> I don't really mind doing this.
> *Add your own ideas:*

Why we should delegate

Your reasons for not delegating may well be accurate and logical.
You know that it is quicker to do things yourself because you have
watched others take twice as long to do even the simplest task
– and then it's not actually done to the standard that you expect.
Yet these and all the other reasons for not asking others to help out
can be challenged with another point of view, which supports the
advantages of delegating.

> *I could do it more quickly myself.*
> At first, yes, but someone else can learn to do it quickly.

> *It would take too long to show someone else how to do this.*
> If it's an ongoing task, it is worth investing the time to teach
> someone else the ropes.

> *No one will do it as well as I do.*
> Maybe not, but you don't need perfection in everything. Your
> time may well be worth more than having everything just so.

> *No one will do it in exactly the way I want it done.*
> Maybe not, but there could be more than one way of achieving
> a result. Your way might not even be the best.

> *Add your own ideas:*

Delegation and our emotional needs

Many of our excuses for not delegating mask an underlying motive which can be hard to acknowledge. We carry on doing certain tasks, even though they drain our time and could be effectively shared or passed on to someone else, because they fulfil an emotional need. Activities to do with running the house and bringing up children often fall into this category. We may find ourselves doing too much but are reluctant to let go of anything because we have ingrained ideas about our role and our responsibility. Emotional needs that prevent us from delegating include:

> We want to be indispensable.
> We want to be needed.
> We need to feel that we can cope with everything.
> We enjoy being a martyr.
> Fear of the changes that may come when we actually have more time.
> Fear of seeming unable to cope.
> We need to be in control.
> *Add your own ideas:*

Weigh up what you gain from having these needs met against what you will gain from letting go of some of the work you take on.

> *What you will gain:*
> More time and less stress.
> Increased self-respect and respect from others.
> The knowledge that you are behaving sensibly and responsibly.
> You will not feel taken for granted.
> You will encourage children and others to be more responsible.
> You will enable others to discover and develop skills and abilities.
> You will present a positive role model to children and others.
> Work will get done more quickly with more hands on deck.
> Work might be done more enjoyably and creatively as people find tasks that they like doing and are good at.

You are teaching children valuable life skills.
Add your own ideas:

How to delegate

Around the home there are many jobs that could be delegated. Sometimes it's good to hand over the whole of a major task to someone who is up to it and who will enjoy the scope and responsibility. If someone cannot take on the whole of a task, offer them smaller jobs that contribute to the whole. It's good if they can see that their time is being used constructively and where their jobs fit in to the whole picture.

Some jobs can be approached in different ways. You may have got used to your way, and assume that it is the best, but someone else might discover short cuts or other ways of getting as good as or even better results.

Match the person to the task

This is the crucial first step in delegation. If you get this wrong, the project is pretty much doomed to failure. Use your knowledge of people's personalities, talents and preferences. Those who are creative in their chosen fields may like to learn to cook creatively; those who like order in their own small environment (e.g. keep their personal items tidy and well looked after) may like to impose and maintain order in another part of the house. Family members with excess energy to burn could take on heavy cleaning tasks, perhaps set against a timer as a challenge; those who are outgoing with good social skills might be good at finding things out for you, running errands, booking appointments.

Persuade them that the task is worthwhile

The best way forward is to have people take on tasks with at least some willingness. Explain why you want to make this arrangement, and listen to what they say. It's a good idea to begin with the desired outcome.

> 'We need everyone to take a share in keeping the house tidy.'
> 'There are lots of things to do before going away on Saturday, so we need to share out some tasks.'
> 'We need to make sure that the animals' cages are cleaned regularly. How would you feel about being in charge of it? You enjoy playing with them, and I know you're responsible enough to be trusted to do it properly.'

Encourage discussion

Listen to people's reactions, and try to listen for the real feelings behind what they say. You may well get an automatic negative response, but this could mask other attitudes. With family members, it is important to establish a system that is seen to be fair to everyone. Without realizing it, you may have encouraged your family to accept the idea that certain (most) tasks are your job, so you may meet some resistance to an altered perception of your role. Have your assertion skills ready to help you to deal with objections.

Be specific

People need to know what they're letting themselves in for and what you expect. Describe what you want as precisely as you can. Remember that we all interpret things differently, and what you have in mind when you say 'Tidy your room' or 'Empty the dishwasher' or 'Take out the rubbish' might not be quite how the other person sees it. This is where the checklists that we discussed earlier come in handy.

When you can, give a demonstration of what you mean. Show how you would like clothes folded, what you want on a table when it's set for a meal, how the pots and pans fit in the cupboard. Make sure everyone knows when and where the bins or recycling boxes should be out for collection.

Prepare to be flexible

At the same time, don't expect too much. You will have your own standards about cleanliness and tidiness, but you may have to relax and accept a less than perfect job. Don't expect too much too soon, either. Give people time to get used to this new routine.

Remember the doubling-up principle. Someone may be persuaded to take on a task if you can show that it could contain added value. You might offer to pay your children to do certain chores, or you might buy their co-operation with treats. Another thing you could do is suggest that the job may have hidden advantages:

- A friend can come along and help – this might lead naturally to a social activity, which you need not present as a condition of the work being done.
- Tasks involving physical activity burn calories and are good for overall fitness.
- Once the bedroom is clear and tidy you will be able to make a decision as to what kind of new decor would work.
- If someone takes on cooking a meal one evening a week, they could invite friends round and cook for them.

Tasks no one likes doing

There are some jobs that everyone tries to avoid because they are just tedious. Most don't take long, but even when you do all you can to distract yourself or pleasantly occupy your mind while you tackle them, it's hard to summon up the will to do so. Simple repetitive jobs like emptying the dishwasher come into this category. It's a routine chore that gets left until you want a cup of coffee and there are no clean cups – and even then, we tend just to grab what we need and leave the rest.

These tasks are good candidates for sharing or delegating. Openly acknowledge that no one is likely to volunteer for these jobs, but they have to be done. Suggest that the fairest thing is for everyone to take a turn. Some jobs might be made more bearable if people do them together. (See Exercise 6.2, p. 88.)

Delegate nice things

Remember to share round the pleasanter tasks as well as the more burdensome ones. People might enjoy checking out a suitable place for a family celebration, doing some of the spade-work to identify a good holiday location, planning and shopping for interesting meals.

Exercise 6.2: Delegating the boring jobs

Make a list of the boring jobs that have to be done. If appropriate, include work and home tasks. Decide what you will do to make sure that you don't end up doing them yourself.

At home:

_____

_____

_____

Action:

_____

_____

_____

At work:

_____

_____

_____

Action:

_____

_____

_____

Remember to show appreciation

Saying thank you is important. Comment on how well something has been done and how much you value the contribution.

Delegation as exchange

Exchanging services

Think of delegating as a joint venture. It's all about co-operation. You may ask someone to do a job for you, and they in turn can 'delegate' back to you when appropriate. Sometimes we are reluctant to network with each other in this time-saving way because of embarrassment or lack of confidence, or fear that our request will be misunderstood.

Emma asks for help
Emma knows that Allie is going to the shop to get a sandwich. The sandwich shop is right next to the chemist, which Emma needs to visit to collect a prescription before the end of the day. Emma's been fretting about how she will find the time to leave her desk. It occurs to Emma that she could ask Allie to pick up the prescription for her, but she doesn't like to in case Allie thinks it is a bit off that she asked.

Emma could work on developing the personal and communication skills that would help her to get Allie's help, and show that she is happy to reciprocate. Given the busy lives we all lead, it is a shame not to make the greatest use of the resources available to help us do everything we have to. For example, it may be possible to ask a family member, friend, or neighbour to let the plumber or electrician in, if it is difficult for you to be at home. In return, you would have to be willing to give up time to reciprocate. That shouldn't be a problem – there are lots of suggestions in Chapter 9 about how to use waiting time profitably. If you and others in your circle have pets, you could take it in turns to bulk buy and deliver pet food to each other. Or you could share out trips to ferry rubbish to the recycling centre, and so on.

Exchanging skills

If you can think of a skill you have, something that you do quickly and easily, that might be useful to someone else, you could offer this service to them in exchange for having something done for you that you find unenjoyable and time-consuming (see Exercise 6.3).

> Lori makes great cakes. She is very happy to bake Deena a cake for her son's eighteenth birthday, and what she produces is better than anything Deena would be able to buy. One thing Lori hates doing is filling in forms – they flummox her, and she always makes mistakes. Deena finds dealing with paperwork easy, and she is happy to do this task for Lori.

Exercise 6.3: Skill swap

Note down the skills you have and tasks you are good at and can offer to others, together with those tasks you find difficult or would prefer not to do, which someone could do for you in exchange.

Other people's skills I would like to use	Skills I can offer in exchange
1	
2	
3	
4	
5	
6	

Buying time

It may be worth paying the right person to do certain time-consuming or less enjoyable tasks for you. There are a host of services on offer. You can find people to clean, to garden, to iron, to decorate, to clear your household junk, to walk your dog, to feed your cat, to shop for you, to cater for your dinner party, to prepare documents and CVs for you, to sell things for you on eBay, to do little odd jobs around the house. You can even get people to come in and organize your cupboards and wardrobes, not to mention your life.

Time versus money

Of course, before paying someone for services, consider the balance of time and money. Is it worth the sum you have to pay to be relieved of this particular task so you are able to spend the time on something else? (See Exercise 6.4.)

Exercise 6.4: Buying time

This exercise will help you to decide if it is worth your while to buy in help. Choose three tasks that you would particularly like to be rid of, and weigh up the costs and benefits of farming them out to someone else.

Task: _____
What the cost would be: _____
How much time I would save: _____
What I would do with the reclaimed time: _____

Task: _____
What the cost would be: _____
How much time I would save: _____
What I would do with the reclaimed time: _____

Task: _____
What the cost would be: _____
How much time I would save: _____
What I would do with the reclaimed time: _____

Where to find help

Local newspapers and newsagents' windows are good places to spot people advertising their services. You could also put in a card of your own describing the service that you need. Here are some other sources you might consider:

- Retired and semi-retired people living locally may have the kinds of skills and experience you are looking for.
- Family, extended family and friends – nephews, nieces, cousins and their friends, your friends' children.
- Local teenagers may be willing to do chores and errands.
- If there is a college or university nearby, some students might be pleased to earn a bit of cash.
- You might find the person you are looking for through a church, school or local newsletter.
- Your network of friends and acquaintances.

You might want to put your request for help, even from a personal friend or acquaintance, on a professional footing by negotiating a fee for services rendered. We sometimes feel shy about doing this, but if you know and trust someone to do a good job, explore this avenue. The advantage of putting a service outside a 'favour' context is that you can always ask for it to be repeated.

Tasks you might pay someone to do

> Ironing
> House cleaning
> Shopping
> Cooking
> Gardening
> Decorating
> Cleaning the car
> Walking the dog when no one else can do it
> Feeding the cat when no one else can do it
> Meeting a child from school
> Taking a child to school
> Organizing your accounts
> Book-keeping
> Odd jobs around the house
> Teach you how to make the best use of your computer
> *Add your own ideas:*

7

How to stop putting things off

Putting off doing something that we know we will have to deal with sooner or later is never a good idea. It's fine to defer something because you need time to think, or want to be sure that you have everything you need to go ahead with an activity, but constantly finding excuses for not tackling a task is a poor use of your time. Often what happens when you do finally get round to it is that either you are pleasantly surprised at how easy it was and regret putting it off, or you have delayed for so long that what might have been easy has become problematic.

There is little logic in the way that we do some tasks readily but constantly defer others. You may find that you have no problem in applying yourself to compiling figures for work, but it takes you a week to get round to cleaning the dish with the burnt-on cheese sauce. Oddly, sometimes we also put off activities that we really want to do, things that concern our personal lives and relationships, that are to do with our big picture goals, but at the same time we manage to start and finish projects that are not essential to our lives and well-being.

Why we procrastinate

Why do so many of us find it difficult to get going on not only the tasks we have to do, but also the things that we want to do as well? And why, once we do make a start, do we become distracted by the slightest thing, or grab at any excuse to stop what we are doing (see Exercise 7.1)? We can find all kinds of excuses:

I'm not in the right mood.
I haven't got everything I need.
It's too difficult.
It's not worth starting it now because there's hardly time to get anything done.
If I ignore it it will go away.

I can always do it later.
There are all these other things to do.
I'm too busy to start that.
It will take too long.
There's no deadline so there's no rush.
I function best when I'm under pressure.

Exercise 7.1: How do you procrastinate?

Think of three things that you have put off doing. Identify the reasons that you give.

What I put off   *Reason I give*

1 _____   _____

2 _____   _____

3 _____   _____

Underlying reasons for procrastination

Sometimes the reasons we give mask the true ones. Our reluctance or inability to get certain things done can be associated with our own personalities, needs and beliefs.

Fear and anxiety

These emotions are at the root of much of our reluctance to tackle things. All kinds of projects and activities are shelved because of inner doubts and fears. Fear of failing at something, or feeling that it's not worth starting because we will never see it through, can stop us putting our plans into action.

Fear of failure

Livvy wants to start a personal fitness plan. She would feel healthier and happier if she took more exercise and ate sensibly. She tried this before and didn't persevere, and the fear that the same thing will happen again and that she will feel a failure stops Livvy from putting her plan into practice.

Maria is having problems with one of her team members whose work has become unsatisfactory. Maria knows that she must speak to him about the situation, but she keeps putting it off, telling herself that he will probably improve and she that she should not rock the boat. Really, she is anxious about her ability to handle the interview effectively.

Fear of success

Strangely enough, fear of accomplishing a task can be as great a barrier as fear of failure. Finishing a project means that something in your life will change, and adjusting to the change can be difficult. If it is a major project, there is likely to be a gap in your life that it once occupied. When the house is decorated and furnished exactly as you want it to be, after you have actually taken that trip of a lifetime and are back home again, what do you do with your free evenings and weekends?

If you succeed in your diet and fitness regime, you will probably experience change in your habits and lifestyle, possibly in ways that were difficult to foresee. Not only you, but others in your life may have to adjust to your new self-image.

If you actually apply for that new job you are always talking about, you have to face the fact that you might get it. Then you will have to deal with the changes in your working life and maybe your personal life that this may involve.

Fear of consequences

We might put off making a doctor's appointment because we are anxious about the outcome of the visit. The same may be true of, for example, making an appointment with your child's school to discuss a problem, or talking to a friend or family member about a personal issue. These situations fall into the 'perhaps it will go away' category, a hope that we cling on to because we shrink from the possible consequences of the task.

Feeling overwhelmed

When a task seems time-consuming, difficult or complicated, we tend to put it off.

Lorri's loft
One of Lorri's home improvement plans is to convert the loft into a third bedroom. The loft has been used as a storage space for anything that needed a home, and is absolutely crammed with stuff. Lorri needs to go through it herself and sort out what should be kept and what should be thrown away, but every time she opens the door and looks at it she feels the need for a cup of coffee or she remembers a phone call she has to make, and goes away again. Meanwhile, the plan to convert the loft gets pushed further and further into the distance.

Wanting it done perfectly

Sometimes we delay starting an activity because we feel that it must be done just right, that there is no margin for error and only 100 per cent perfection is acceptable. We get ourselves out of this trap by finding reasons for delaying – I need more information, I need to be in exactly the right frame of mind, I need to be absolutely sure that it is going to work, I need to do more research. We put the task off for so long that in the end we may have to do it in a hurry, thereby giving ourselves the excuse that we did not have time to do a good job.

Staying within our comfort zone

Sometimes hanging on to a dream is comforting – the idea that 'one day' we will learn to paint, or dance, or horse ride, or take a trip to a country we have always longed to visit, or build an extension to the house, or apply for promotion. Even a routine that we do not particularly enjoy has the advantage of being familiar, and at least we feel safe and know where we are with it.

Getting the priority wrong

Sometimes tasks hang about because getting them done isn't really all that important. Although they may have been of consequence to you once, circumstances have changed; or maybe they never were very important, but you have just got into the habit of thinking that they were.

How to overcome procrastination

When you are clear in your mind that the task that you are putting off is important and has to be done, and that the consequences of doing it out outweigh the consequences of not doing it (see Exercise 7.2, p. 96), try some of these strategies for getting going. Choose methods that you think will work for you.

Break up the task into single actions

No matter how huge the project, reduce it to a list of actions. Some of these will probably need to be consecutive, and dealing with one may depend on having completed something else, but there will be small stand-alone tasks that can be done at any time. Once you have your list, you can decide when to undertake the actions.

Exercise 7.2: Facing up to procrastination

Decide what the real reason is for your delay in three particular tasks. Then think about the likely consequences if the task never gets done. Weigh these against the benefits of actually doing it.

Example
What I'm putting off:
Applying for another job.

Reason for delaying:
I'm scared that I will be unsuccessful. I know the set-up and the people in my current job, and feel comfortable with them.

If I continue to delay:
I will carry on being bored and frustrated because there is no scope for me to use my skills.

If I take the plunge:
I will probably get what I want, even if it takes a while. The process will be good experience. I don't actually have to accept anything I am not sure about.

1 What I'm putting off: _____
Reason for delaying: _____
If I continue to delay: _____
If I take the plunge: _____

2 What I'm putting off: _____
Reason for delaying: _____
If I continue to delay: _____
If I take the plunge: _____

3 What I'm putting off: _____
Reason for delaying: _____
If I continue to delay: _____
If I take the plunge: _____

Tanika is responsible for producing the monthly newsletter. Instead of thinking in terms of 'the newsletter', a task that is hanging over her like a dark cloud, she writes a list of all the individual actions associated with the job. Her list includes items such as:

Email Tom for details of ramble.
Ask George to take on diary slot.
Arrange meeting with Sophie to discuss budget increase.

Tanika's newsletter
Tanika can slot in the items on her list at appropriate times. None of these single actions is in itself daunting, and will not take very long. Of course, other actions will be more time-consuming, but when some things are easily dealt with and ticked off the list, the whole task seems less overwhelming, and Tanika feels that she is making progress.

Try this process with large projects such as moving house, organizing parties and weddings, sorting out schools for children. The thought of the whole process is overwhelming and leads you to delay starting, but individual actions such as 'Phone three estate agents', 'Phone three venues', 'Go to the library to find out the names of the schools in the area' are manageable.

Do it straight away

If an action will genuinely take only a few minutes, do it right now. This is a good strategy for actions which fall into the 'fear of consequences' category. If you know you have to do it, and it only takes a phone call, stop worrying about it and just make the call. Now.

Divide the task into time units

Decide how much time you need to devote to the task, and plan to spend an appropriate unit of time per day, or per week, or whatever you need, until you get it done. Just half an hour a day adds up. Make the units of time short and manageable so that you do not get disheartened. A lot can be achieved in 15 minutes, particularly if you know that this is the only time available. It may help to commit yourself to a certain number of units at one go, and give yourself permission to stop after that time is up. You can choose to add on another unit if you wish, but you don't have to. You can make this work with time slots of just five minutes.

Do the most unpleasant or difficult task first

It is always good to get something difficult out of the way. If there are lots of unpleasant things to do, think about offloading some of them (see Chapter 6). Otherwise, alternate tasks you don't like doing with things that you enjoy.

Set yourself start times

What you do is commit yourself to doing something on a certain day. It may help to decide when in the day you are going to begin the task. This sometimes works better than setting a deadline.

Chronic procrastinators can fool themselves that they will meet a deadline up until the moment that it has passed.

Tie the task into your body clock

If you put a task off because you are too tired to deal with it, decide to tackle it at a time of the day when you have the energy to do it effectively and quickly. Tie the task into your emotional state. For instance, make use of the surge of energy you feel when you are worked up about something. Channel this into the task you have been putting off. In giving vent to the intensity of your feelings, you may find that you have managed to clean the bathroom thoroughly in no time at all!

Control your 'getting going' habits

Little routines that you feel you have to complete before you actually get on with a task can become very time-consuming. Making one cup of coffee is fine, but if you then have to straighten things around the room, water the plants, check your text messages and emails just in case, have a go at the quick crossword just to get your brain working, then you need to kick your habit. Try removing the distractions. Hide the remote control. Put that inviting magazine outside the door or under the bed. Turn your chair away from the window or the corridor so that you can't see what's going on. Cut yourself off from interruptions. Don't answer the phone, or get drawn into conversations.

Give yourself rewards

Having got going, fix a few points at which you can congratulate yourself on achieving something. You need not wait until you have finished the whole task. Build in rewards for completing certain stages of what you have to do.

Involve other people

Going public can be a great help. If appropriate people know what you are doing, you are likely to feel motivated to get on with it. You could ask people to jog you along with the occasional enquiry as to how it's going.

Frame the task to suit your needs

When a task is getting you down, try to look at the task in another way. If it hangs over you like a cloud, lift the cloud by finding an entertaining way to get it done. Some ideas might be:

- Play music to help you along.
- Get a friend involved and tackle it together.
- Tie it in with something that is nice to do.

Putting fun into chores

Kirsty needs to blitz the garden and the yard, a task she has been putting off because it is such arduous work. She decides to rope in friends and family, as many as she can persuade, and combines a garden-clearing day with a barbecue.

Bonnie needs to take her car in for a routine service, but puts off making arrangements for getting the car to her garage. She suggests to her friend Terri that they drive over together then go for a pub lunch.

Exercise 7.3: Planning to do it now

Choose three of the tasks or projects that you are putting off. Decide which strategies you will use to get going on them. Make a plan.

1 Task: _____
How I will start it: _____
Start date: _____
Action steps: _____

2 Task: _____
How I will start it: _____
Start date: _____
Action steps: _____

3 Task: _____
How I will start it: _____
Start date: _____
Action steps: _____

8

Strategies and tips for different personality types

Effective time management is based on planning and organization – words that some of us shy away from. Not everyone is a natural organizer, and not everyone relishes the process of planning and ordering their life. However, the basic techniques of managing time can be adapted to suit different needs and personalities.

Managing time when you don't like planning

You may be one of those people who are resistant to the very idea of planning. You think that planning takes away life's spontaneity. You fear that you will become controlled, trapped by a list of tasks that you are obliged to do. Or you may start to plan, then lose heart because you get bogged down in the process. At this point you abandon the planning process and forge ahead, or you abandon what you were doing.

The main advantage to being a non-planner is that things do tend to get done, because you are likely to get on with them rather than sit around planning. The disadvantage is that lack of planning can result in activities being rushed and perhaps botched, because you haven't thought things through sufficiently. Strategies to encourage you to plan might include:

- *Use your imagination to spark the planning process.* Try visualizing yourself on the planning path. You could even actually draw it as a path. Fill in the roadblocks that stop you making progress.
- *Turn planning into a game.* Draw a games board with squares and fill in the steps you need to take, showing the direction of your progress and how you might deal with any obstacles that you encounter.
- *Ask a friend.* If you cannot see a clear way to achieving your outcome, talk it over with someone who can ask you the right questions and make helpful suggestions.
- *Make a comprehensive 'to do' list.* Aim for the kind of list that we

looked at earlier. Writing down absolutely everything that you need to get done clears your mind remarkably, as if the act of putting it all on paper, or on a screen, unburdens you. It also gives you an overview of the project or activity, and enables you to group together related items. Choose one action to do first, and build up from there.

Managing time when you're a disorganized person

You might find the whole concept of time difficult – you are always late, or you get carried away with what you are doing and time just runs away with you. Or perhaps you just can't think in the kind of linear way that supports organization. If you tend to live in the minute and hate the idea of following a schedule, try some of these approaches:

- *Stop what you are doing for a few seconds.* Concentrate on the minute, and ask yourself if you are making the best use of your time at this moment.
- *Work with your surges of energy.* Develop a rhythm of working in short bursts to stop yourself getting bored.
- *Visualize your ultimate goal.* If you leave things to the last minute, keep yourself focused on what you aim to achieve. You don't want to turn up at the birthday party without a present, or to spoil the special dinner you are cooking because you forgot to pick up a vital ingredient, or miss your flight at the start of your holiday. Apply the process that helps you to plan for special events to other occasions as well.

Right brainers and left brainers

If you dislike planning, organizing and making lists, it is possible that you are someone who has 'right-brain dominance'. Different parts of the human brain are responsible for different kinds of thinking. The left-hand sections of the brain process information in a logical, orderly way, whereas the right-hand sections produce thinking that is more random and creative. Many of us prefer one of these styles of thinking over the other, and have grown used to processing information using our preferred side.

Your preference affects the way that you manage your time. If your left brain is dominant, you are probably very comfortable with making lists and planning; if you are a right-brained person, you may find that way of organizing yourself difficult and not to your taste. It is helpful to develop the ability to use both modes, exploiting the strengths and advantages of each. Of course, you

---

Exercise 8.1: Discover your preference

		Yes	No	Sometimes
1	I think there is a right way and a wrong way of doing things.	____ ____	____ ____	_____ _____
2	I don't like sticking to a schedule or routine.	____	____	_____
3	I prefer non-fiction books to fiction.	____	____	_____
4	I use my hands a lot when I talk.	____	____	_____
5	I read instruction manuals before getting an appliance to work.	____	____	_____
6	I can tell if someone is lying by just looking at them.	____	____	_____
7	I like to keep things neat and uncluttered.	____	____	_____
8	I often rely on my gut instinct.	____	____	_____
9	I am persuaded by facts and figures rather than by emotional appeals.	____	____	_____
10	I like completing tasks and ticking them off a list.	____	____	_____
11	I find that time passes without my noticing.	____	____	_____
12	If someone asks me for directions, I like to draw a map rather than explain the way.	____	____	_____

If you answered 'yes' to questions 1, 3, 5, 7, 9 and 10 you show some of the characteristics of left-brain thinkers. If you answered 'yes' to questions 2, 4, 6, 8, 11 and 12 you show some of the characteristics of right-brain thinkers. If your answers indicate a mixture, you may have a holistic or whole-brained way of thinking, and can access both ways of thinking.

may already be well balanced in this respect, and show character-istics from each area (see Exercise 8.1).

Left brainers enjoy the aspects of time management that reflect their liking for order and organization. You like logical plans and regimes, and are good at following procedures. Ways of making your preference work for you include:

- *Make full use of lists, forms and schedules.* You enjoy using them, and get satisfaction from completing items. You could fine-tune your 'to do' list, specifying precise times for some activities.
- *Use headings and subheadings to order your notes.* Employ electronic gadgets as your organizing tools. You might enjoy the step-by-step process of entering and retrieving information, which appeals to your sense of order and logic.
- *Apply your planning skills to all areas of your life.* Your liking for detail might cause you to lose sight of the big picture.
- *Build in buffer time.* You may feel anxious when your plans are interrupted or the unexpected occurs. Allow yourself more time than you know you need.
- *Understand that other people may organize their lives differently.* People you work or live with may have approaches to tasks that seem to you to be sloppy and unfocused. Try to see the outcomes rather than the ways of achieving them.
- *Try to be flexible.* It's possible you might become a bit rigid in your approach to time. Accept that hitches and changes of plan are bound to occur. It need not be the end of the world if your schedule is disrupted – you are quite capable of adapting to events. In fact, you might experience benefits in seeing things differently or having to go in a new direction.

Right brainers like the big picture. They like to see the whole, then look at the parts, while left brainers start with the parts and build up to the whole. They also like to see the picture in colour. If this is you, try drawing mind maps or diagrams instead of lists. Use colours and illustrations to make them vibrant and personal. You can use maps for:

> 'To do' lists
> Planning aids for projects
> Decision-making aids
> Shopping guides

Study or learning aids
Add your own ideas:

Sometimes people who don't like lists are the ones who need them most. It is particularly important for you to use appealing notebooks and materials for writing things down. Other ideas include:

- *Write items on index cards instead of making lists.* Put one item on each card, then play around with them, shuffling them into an appropriate order.
- *Put reminders where you can see them.* You could use coloured stick-on notes and attach them round your computer, on the wall, in your notebook. It might be a good idea to put up only the notes that refer to that day, and remember to take the reminders down when you have completed an item.
- *Combine the two systems.* Use sticky notes, but keep them together in a notebook or file. It's a good idea to keep lists and reminders in one place.
- *Choose calendars and planners that you like.* They might need to be bright and fun to use, ones that you find aesthetically pleasing. You could make your own.
- *Visualize the outcomes that you want.* Make the big picture bright and glowing, and see yourself in the centre of it.
- *Use clocks and timers to remind you of time passing.* You may tend to forget about time and immerse yourself in the moment. Try setting a buzzer to go every half an hour, and ask yourself how your actions in the last half-hour have contributed to your goals.
- *Concentrate on one major project at a time.* To help you focus on a particular task, imagine that you are wearing blinkers so that you are unable to see anything else. Concentrate on the things that are important to you, and direct your activities to these goals.
- *Think about the order in which you do things.* Rather than put off tasks that you find routine and boring, alternate them with activities that you enjoy more.
- *Team up with someone who likes order and systems.*

Managing time if you're a perfectionist

Perfectionists like to excel at what they do, but they find it very difficult to manage their time effectively. They become so focused on things being exactly right that they lose their sense of perspective. The big picture becomes obscured as so much time and energy are devoted to details that often do not merit such close attention. Being driven by a desire to be perfect in all that you do can lead to your actually achieving very little. You dread falling short of your own high standards and fear letting yourself down.

If the following statements reflect the way that you think, it is quite likely that you fall into the perfectionist category.

> 'There's no point in doing something unless you get it absolutely right.'
> 'I pride myself on paying attention to detail.'
> 'I need to do things myself because then I know that they are done properly.'

Think about trying to estimate how much time and attention activities really need. Not everything needs to be 100 per cent perfect. Some things will, of course, benefit from your highly developed skills and your attention to detail. But if you take a more relaxed approach to the other tasks that constitute the bulk of your activities, you will free up time for yourself and conserve your energy for matters that do need your perfectionist skills.

Change your thinking. Train yourself to challenge the thoughts that trap you in misplaced perfectionism. Instead of:

> 'I must give this 100 per cent.'
> 'This must be exactly right down to the last detail.'

Try saying to yourself:

> 'I'll give this a good shot.'
> 'I'll make this good enough for what's required.'
> 'Just because I can find or have all this information doesn't mean that it is necessary or appropriate to give it in such detail.'

Set yourself deadlines. Be firm with yourself and limit the amount of time that you spend on things. Ask yourself what would happen if you produce a less-than-perfect result. Use delegation to help you loosen up a little. Accept someone else's lack of perfection.

9

Making technology work for you

Using the telephone

The phone can be both a great time-saver and a great time-waster. Telephone time needs to be managed effectively so that it works for us rather than against us. Sometimes you want a long chat on the phone, but at other times you just want to give or receive information as quickly as possible. If you find that time runs away with you when you are on the phone, try asking yourself before each call: What am I making this call for?

If you are chatting with a friend, try to allocate the amount of time you want to be on the phone beforehand. It's useful to make clear the point of your call at the beginning of the conversation. This gives the other person an opportunity to indicate if it is a good time for them. If you are phoning for a specific purpose, make that clear at the beginning of the call too. It isn't rude to get to the point; in fact, it shows respect for the other person's time as well as your own. If you make a quick call to a friend for a piece of information or to confirm a date, finish the call by saying something like, 'I'll phone later in the week for a proper chat.'

If you are phoning someone with a request for information, be absolutely clear about what you want to know and write down the questions that you want to ask. Have with you any papers that you might need to refer to.

When you leave a message for someone to call back, in order to avoid a time-wasting string of messages and attempts to make contact, specify when you will be available to take the call. Make your message clear, and give relevant information.

Have your most regularly used numbers on speed dial, or keep them near the phone.

When someone phones you, they will have no way of knowing what your situation or your mood is at that very moment. They don't know if you have two minutes or two hours available. It's up to you to let the person know if you are not able to chat. With friends and people you know well, there are a number of phrases you can use that make the situation clear and which you should be comfortable using.

Samantha's phone management

Jenni calls Samantha early one evening. 'Glad I've found you in!' she says. 'Just wait until you hear what happened today!'

'I'd love to hear about it,' Samantha says, 'but I can't chat properly right now. Can I call you back later?'

With people you know less well, or work colleagues, try a friendly but crisp, 'How can I help you?' or 'What can I do for you?' This encourages the person to come straight to the point and cuts out preliminary chit-chat.

You might choose to let your machine or message service take the call, and return it at a time convenient for you. It can be hard not to answer a ringing phone, but if you make yourself always available you can lose control of your time. However, treat the voice mail facility with caution. You may end up spending ages returning calls. Again, when someone is going to call you back, let them know times when you will be available to speak.

Top time-saving tip for phone calls

Have a pen and notebook handy and take notes as you speak. Keep materials by the phone for this purpose. If you use a desk diary then make your phone call notes on the appropriate page. Doing this avoids all the 'Just go over the address again' types of exchange. It has other side benefits as well. You build up a record of various pieces of information that are communicated in personal and work-related talk, and you can flip back through the pages of your notebook to remind yourself of addresses, numbers and the name of your friend's cousin's new baby.

Tame your mobile phone

Somehow it seems to be harder to manage mobile phone calls than it is to deal with landline calls. Try to stay in control of your phone, rather than have it control you. You don't *have* to answer your phone every time it rings. Trying to conduct a conversation in difficult circumstances can be a real time-waster as you end up having to repeat the same details at another time. You can actually *turn it off,* and just check for messages at certain times, as you do with emails. If people have constant access to you and expect immediate responses, you are in effect handing over your time to them.

Think about how much time you spend texting. By constantly sending and replying to unnecessary messages you are getting locked into a cycle of frittering away time. On the other hand, texting to make and confirm arrangements is a great time-saver, and stops you getting involved in phone calls that drift on.

Make full use of your mobile phone

You may already use your phone to take photographs or send and receive emails and voice mails. Find out all the things that your mobile phone can do. Many phones have WAP (Wireless Application Protocol), which makes them like mini-computers. Decide which of its applications would save you time and hassle.

Using your computer

Getting in control of emails

A good way of dealing with email overload is to think of the messages as paper communications and deal with them in the same way. When you read a memo or open a letter, you are unlikely to drop everything that you are doing and send off an immediate response. You think about how you want to reply, and you almost instinctively judge the appropriate time within which to answer. Try to do the same with emails. The speed and nature of this type of communication set up expectations of immediate feedback, but you will find that you can break this cycle by the way that you handle email exchanges.

Switch off the device that alerts you to new messages. Instant handling of messages may give the illusion that you are saving time by dealing with things immediately, but in fact reading and replying to emails as they arrive is not a good use of time. Doing this makes you lose sight of your own priorities, allowing matters to rise to the top of your list just because they have been emailed to you. Being sent by email does not automatically make a message urgent or important.

Set aside a time slot for doing emails. (Use the ideas in Chapter 3 about choosing time slots for particular activities.) Delete spam mail immediately. Don't open it just to check that it really is unsolicited communication – it will be. Find out about the programmes which will block unwanted messages.

Set up a file or folder in which you can store emails and attachments in the same way that you store paperwork. Devise a system that works for you – your various folders might be labelled 'To do', 'Friends', or 'Checklists', for the lists we discussed earlier. Drag items that you need to do something about straight into an 'Action' folder. In this way your in-box is kept free and you are saved from scrolling through pages of messages to find the one that you want.

Ask yourself if it would be easier and quicker to respond in person rather than send back an email. Lengthy or complicated matters may be more effectively and speedily handled in conversation. When writing an email you are entirely dependent on the words you use to get your message across, and it is alarmingly easy to get the tone wrong or use the wrong expression. The misunderstandings this can cause may take ages to sort out. Face to face or on the phone you have a chance to check how your message is being received and to put right immediately any misunderstandings that occur.

Sometimes writing a reply on paper is more appropriate than sending an email. Maybe you could just jot down a few words in response to a document you've received, on the document itself, and send it back.

Limit the number of emails you send, and this will limit the number that you receive. Don't automatically copy in everybody you can think of, whether it is to share a joke or pass on news or items of information. Ask yourself if the communication is relevant to everyone, and if you would still send it if there was no email and you had to communicate it by some other means. Cut down on unnecessary exchanges by making it clear whether or not a reply is needed, and don't get locked into a long cycle of thanks and acknowledgements.

Using the Internet

Finding information on the World Wide Web, and buying items online, can be great time-savers. This won't be the case, however, if your intention is to find a cheap flight to Barcelona and you become distracted by the handbags on eBay. Learn to search purposefully, and bookmark the sites you use all the time.

Make your request for information as specific as possible. Remember that you will get results for every word you enter. Put + in front of a word that you want included, and inverted commas around whole phrases. Experiment with different search engines to find the ones that suit your needs.

If you want to control the amount of time you spend looking things up, set an alarm to alert you that you have been on for a period of, say, 30 minutes.

How your computer can save you time

Your PC can enable you to do many useful tasks from your home, including:

> Online banking and payment of bills
> Compile and maintain your address/contact list
> Store important information
> Scan, print and send photos, articles, recipes, copies of letters
> Do your diary
> Book holidays
> Find a job

However, using your computer for these activities can also take a lot of time. Before you go all-electronic, think about the time investment needed in learning how to use the systems properly, and how far your PC will help you to manage your time and your tasks effectively. You will save time if you:

● Regularly back up your files.
● Delete files and programs you no longer use.
● Find out and use the short cuts on your keyboard.
● Get into habits that will avoid frustrating and time-wasting rescue jobs later. Save your work regularly, so that even if your system collapses, there is a chance that your file can be retrieved.

Suggestions for avoiding wasting time:

● Don't spend ages playing around with typefaces and fonts, just because they are there.
● Try not to edit and re-edit work when there is no need to.
● Don't play games instead of doing other tasks.

- Avoid chat rooms – they are addictive.
- Don't produce and present more information than is strictly necessary.

Top time-saving tip for getting the most out of your computer

Go on a course to learn how to make the best use of your computer's functions. It will be worth the investment of time and money. If you don't feel like committing yourself to a formal course, look out for adverts in shop windows and local papers for individual computer tuition in your home. Another idea would be to pay a family member or neighbour to give you a few lessons.

Electronic organizers

Notebook-sized computers like BlackBerrys and PalmPilots perform a range of functions and tasks quickly and on the spot. You don't need to be sitting in front of a computer but can use this digital tool any time, anywhere, so you can make full use of your time. Handheld computers of this kind can be used as you would a paper notebook, for entering and storing information (huge amounts of information, unlike an ordinary planner), and have the added functions that you find on a PC. They can be synchronized with your desktop PC so that you have all the information you need at your fingertips. If you like using technology, this kind of time management aid may be just the thing for you.

Top time-saving tip for electronic and other gadgets

Learn a bit about how they work and how to fix them. When machines, gadgets and appliances go wrong, sometimes all you can do is endure the frustrations of waiting for someone to put them right. For the little hitches that regularly occur, it is worth investing some time in learning how to fix them.

It might be a good idea to keep quiet about your knowledge, to stem the flood of requests for help that are bound to come your way once you are known to be an expert at fixing the photocopier or getting the system network going again.

10

Three golden rules for finding more time

1 Use small amounts of time

Many days contain little pockets of time when nothing is going on. You're waiting for an appointment, or for the plumber or electrician to arrive, you're stuck in traffic, your train or bus is late, you're sitting in your car while your child has a half-hour music lesson, you've been put on hold on the phone ... Rather than feel impatient and irritated, be prepared to use these little amounts of time in ways that make you feel good that you have done something of your choice.

How to use waiting time

- *Regenerate and refresh.* Take a moment for yourself. You don't have to be doing something every minute of the day. It's a great idea to use unexpected minutes and between times to do something for your own well-being. Try relaxation exercises and deep breathing. You could meditate, or daydream. Depending on the context, you could even close your eyes and just rest.
- *Personal grooming tasks.* The time spent waiting to pick up the kids or for people to get ready could be an opportunity to do your nails or your eyebrows. If you regularly spend waiting time in your car, keep a little manicure kit in the glove compartment.
- *Read.* These moments may be opportunities to read a chapter of a book, or a magazine article, or information sheets. Get into the habit of always having something to read on you, and you will be surprised how much you can get through by using waiting time in this way.
- *Use your notebook.* Keep your notebook with you, the one in which you make your lists. Jot down plans and ideas, or reminders, or review your 'to do' list. Or you could just doodle and let ideas float to the surface of your mind.

- *Listen to music.* Here's an opportunity to listen to something of your own choice, rather than what other people want. Or just have it as background.
- *Listen to the radio.* Experiment with different stations and find something that suits you. Decide to listen for 15 minutes to a new station every week – you might make an enjoyable discovery.
- *Play audio books or tapes.* This is a painless way of becoming familiar with subjects that interest you. Over the course of a week or so you could have taken in that chunky novel that is too bulky to carry around, or have learnt some French or Italian.
- *Talk to people.* If you're waiting at your child's school, rather than immerse yourself in a book, chat to other parents. Increasing your network of friends and people with similar interests or in a similar situation to yourself not only enhances your social contact, it can also lead to a better use of time. All kinds of resources can be pooled and shared, freeing up time for everyone concerned.
- *Do puzzles.* Crosswords, codewords, Sudoku and so on are not only enjoyable but can also contribute to your well-being by exercising your mind.
- *Meditate.* This may take a bit of getting used to. Until you are familiar with doing this, keep a little book of meditation exercises in the car or in your bag.
- *Update your phone.* Delete messages, edit numbers, etc.

How to avoid waiting time

Some waiting is always inevitable, but occasionally you can save yourself some time:

- Check road and travel conditions before you set out on a journey.
- Listen to local radio bulletins for traffic delays.
- Check that a flight is on time before you leave to meet someone from an airport.
- Ring to confirm that an appointment will be kept.
- Ring to see if your dentist is running late with appointments.
- Ring to check that your test results have arrived before you go to see your doctor to discuss them.
- Check that an item you want to buy is in stock before going to the shop to purchase it.

Useful things to do while watching television

It depends on the level of concentration required, but for the majority of entertainment programmes you could:

Iron
Sort clothes
Give yourself a manicure/pedicure/face mask
Spruce up your wardrobe by doing minor repairs – sewing on
    buttons, fixing hems
Update your address book
Go through a file and prune papers
Cuddle someone
Stroke your pet
Add your own ideas:

Useful things to do while you're on the telephone

This depends on what kind of phone conversation you are having, and also, of course, on what type of telephone you are speaking on. A hands-free phone opens up time-saving opportunities, but at the same time this can be alienating or off-putting for the other person. The person at the other end of the line will pick up on the fact that you are doing something else as you chat. Use your judgement as to what kind of activity you can do. There is a difference, for example, between talking to someone while you wash up and talking to someone while you are having a bath, between having a conversation while you drink a cup of tea and while you attack your Chinese takeaway. Nifty doubling-up of tasks can save time in one way, but can end up costing you time if you get it wrong and upset the other person in some way.

If you need to listen and concentrate, do something routine and mechanical that doesn't take away your attention. Choose from these suggestions, and add your own.

Iron
Sort clothes
Cook

Prepare packed lunches
Wash up
Give yourself a manicure/pedicure
Clean out your handbag
Clean out your make-up bag
Do some relaxation exercises
Straighten out a drawer
Sort out a file
Do a bit of dusting
Tidy up
Check the weather forecast on teletext

Or you could just put your feet up and have a chat.

What to do while travelling

Read a book, newspaper or magazine
Listen to music
Do puzzles
Work on your lap-top
Jot down ideas in your notebook
Write short notes
Review your 'to do' list
Do deep-breathing and relaxation exercises
Enjoy the scenery
Talk to someone
Sleep

Exercise 10.1: Prepare for waiting time

Decide what item or items you will always carry with you that will help you to use waiting time effectively.

1 _____

2 _____

3 _____

Make up a way of reminding yourself to check that you have these items.

2 Clear as you go

Keeping on top of day-to-day tidying tasks saves time in the long run. If you let things build up, then tackling them becomes a major time commitment. Clearing out the loft or a cupboard, blitzing the kitchen or bathroom, overhauling your whole filing system, are the kinds of task that you need never have to do if you tidy or sort as you go along. You hardly notice the few minutes a day you spend doing this, and you could save, say, a whole Saturday morning. Guidelines for clear as you go include:

> Never put something down, put it where it is kept.
> Rinse cups and mugs immediately or put them straight into the dishwasher.
> Do a daily trawl of newspapers and other items for recycling.
> Hang clothes up right away.
> If items need to be taken upstairs, leave them near the bottom of the stairs. Introduce a system in which no one goes upstairs without taking something from the pile with them.
> Clean round basins and taps when you use them.
> Take a few minutes to clean up spills straight away, and save half an hour of scrubbing later on.
> *Add your own ideas:*

3 Do things in advance

Get ready the night before

A bit of preparation the night before saves time and tempers. Before going to bed, decide and check the clothes you will wear the next day, avoiding last-minute panics of indecision or not being able to find what you want. Mentally review the following day, or look at your 'to do' list. Put in your bag everything you need to take with you. The 'I'll find that in the morning' approach is usually a recipe for disaster. Put your bag somewhere convenient near the door.

Do the same for your children, or encourage them to do it for themselves. Try to have school bags packed, money ready, snacks and packed lunches prepared. A ready-the-night-before system is a form of damage limitation. Nothing on earth will prevent the last-minute demands in the morning to sign a form that has suddenly been discovered at the bottom of a bag, or for money for a trip that you should have been told about weeks ago. But if you prepared as much as possible the night before you are ahead of the game and more able to take these demands in your stride.

Getting ahead for predictable events

We have looked at the advantages of breaking down activities into small tasks. Apply this principle to the inevitable big events that you know will take up time. For example, you know that you will have a certain number of Christmas cards to write, or you know that you have a holiday coming up in the place that you go to every year. Don't do things so far in advance that you feel ridiculous, but when the season draws near, write a few Christmas cards a day (which you can do while you are watching television), or put into your shopping basket the particular insect repellent cream that works for everyone. These actions take just a few minutes and lighten the load when the event is upon you.

Finally

You may have no choice about the number of hours and minutes in a day, but you do have a choice about how to spend them. Apply what you have learnt about time management to make good choices, the kinds of decisions that enable you to live what is the best life for you. Take as much control as you can over the way you spend your time, and don't let the clock take control of you. By putting into practice the ideas and strategies that we have discussed, and making them work for you, you will still be a busy woman, but you will be directing your time and energy to the things that matter most to you.

Further reading

Black, Octavius and Bailey, Sebastian (2006) *The Mind Gym: Give Me Time*, London: Time Warner.

Culp, Stephanie (1995) *You Can Make More Time for Yourself Every Day*, Cincinnati, OH: North Light Books.

Forster, Mark (2005) *Do it Tomorrow*, London: Hodder & Stoughton.

Greene, Mark (2000) *The Which Way to Manage your Time*, London: Which Guides.

Lehmkuhl, Dorothy and Laming, Dolores Cotter (1993) *Organizing for the Creative Person*, London: Kogan Page.

Walter, Dawna (2003) *How To Do Everything and Still Have Time for Yourself*, London: Quadrille.

Index